DATE DUE

DEC. 21	5-20-02	lFEB 2 7	2006
JY 7 '93	6-6-00		JUL 1 7 2006
JA 20 '93			
NO 8	MAY 1 4 2003		NOV 6 2006
FE 8 '94	FEB 1 1 2004		NOV 6 2006
MR 30 '94	FEB 2 3 2004		
NO 9 '94	MAR 1 0 2004		
FEB 1 2 1998			
NOV 6 1998	MAY 0 6 2004		
SEP 1 3 2000	JUN 2 2 2005		
APR 1 8 2002			
MAY 02-02	DEC 2 7 2005		

KNOTS

USEFUL & ORNAMENTAL

KNOTS
USEFUL & ORNAMENTAL

By

GEORGE RUSSELL SHAW

BONANZA BOOKS · NEW YORK

Copyright MCMXXIV, MCMXXXIII by George Russell Shaw
renewed Copyright MCMLI by Francis G. Shaw Jr. and © MCMLX by
Thomas Mott Shaw

This edition is published by Bonanza Books, distributed by Crown Publishers,
Inc., by arrangement with Houghton Mifflin Company.

Manufactured in the United States of America

Library of Congress Cataloging in Publication Data
Shaw, George Russell, b. 1848.
    Knots, useful and ornamental.
    Reprint. Originally published: 2nd ed. Boston:
Houghton, Mifflin, 1933.
    1. Knots and splices.   I. Title.
VW533.S4   1984   623.88'82   84-20424
ISBN: 0-517-460009

h g

INSCRIBED
TO
ROBERT GOULD SHAW
BY HIS
BROTHER

I N the United States, the study of knots has moved westward and may be found in the curriculum of western State Colleges. There the A B seaman, the familiar tar of the deep seas, finds a worthy coadjutor in the Mexican Vaquerro, the mounted Cowboy, skilful in the training of horses, in the embellishment of saddlery, very skilful with the rope, bringing with him names of Spanish origin — lasso, cinch, lariat, latigo hondo — now permanently grafted on the English tongue as it is spoken in all the ranches beyond the Mississippi.

In many details incidental to the care and breeding of stock, to the cultivation of land, to the harvest, its storage and transportation, there are occasions for the use of cordage where the knowledge of reliable knots, appropriate for whatso ever emergency, is an important part of the ranchmans education.

In the first edition, #64 braid of the New Bedford Textile Co. was recommended for practice in tying knots. If the ends when cut, are dipped in paste or rubber cement and are rolled between the fingers, the strands will not unravel and a rigid end will result, very convenient for reeving through eyelets or loops.

CONTENTS

CONTENTS

1
DEFINITIONS

The <u>End</u> of a Line
  is the part that ties the knot
  shown thus
      on the drawings

The Standing Part
  is the rest of the Line
  shown unfinished
      on the drawings
      as at A
    Standing Part

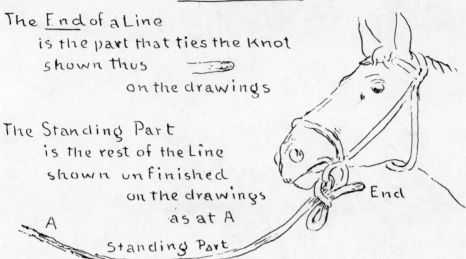

End

A

<u>The</u> Bight is the part of the line between its ends

A Bight

is a more or less pronounced
bend
in a line - Figs. II, a or b

II-a

II-b

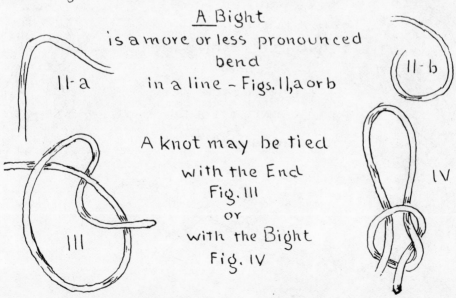

III

A knot may be tied
  with the End
  Fig. III
    or
  with the Bight
  Fig. IV

IV

2

A HITCH

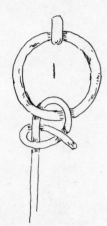

as here understood
is a Knot
tied to a
ring, spar, post, cable
or
other anchorage
not a part of the knot itself
Figs. I, II, III.

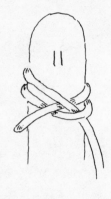

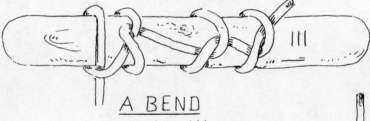

A BEND

is a Knot uniting
two lines
or two parts of the same line
where
each line or each part
is an integral part of the Knot
Figs IV, V, VI.

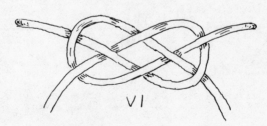

NOOSE and LOOP

A Noose
is tied with
a Hitch
of one of its parts A-A
around the other B~B,
which remains straight. Fig. I

A Loop
is tied with
a Bend
where both parts C & D combine
to form the knot
Fig II

A Noose Fig. I
may become a Loop Fig III
by tying a Hitch
in the
running part B

A Loop Fig II
may become a Noose Fig IV
when one
of its parts C-C-C
can be straightened

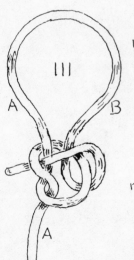

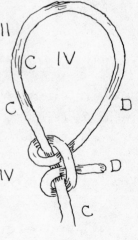

4

HALF HITCH

A round turn of a line about
a post or a spar
One part
of the line
bears or jams upon the other
Figs. I & II

I

II

or

A Turn
of the end of a line
around the
standing part
Figs III, IV

III

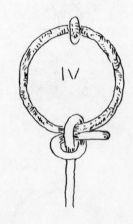

IV

In Fig. V by
pulling B down
and A up
the hitch M
will be
transferred to
the other
part of the line
Fig. VI

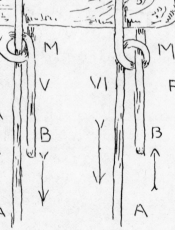

M

V

VI

M

B

B

A

A

In Fig. VI
by
pulling A down
and B up
the hitch M
regains
its original
position

TWO
HALF HITCHES

I
Lark

II
Clove

It will be seen later
that the knot
of
Fig.I-Lark
is a form of the
Reef Knot
page
19
Fig II-Clove
is a form of the
Granny

Page 32

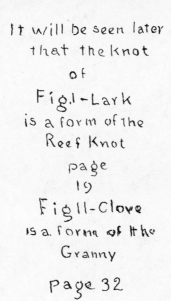

III
Crossed
Lark

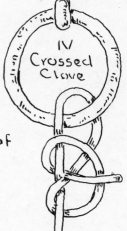

IV
Crossed
Clove

Fig. III- Crossed Lark is
a form of the
Oblique Square Knot
page 20

Fig IV - Crossed Clove, of
the
Oblique Granny
page 33

6

LARK'S HEAD

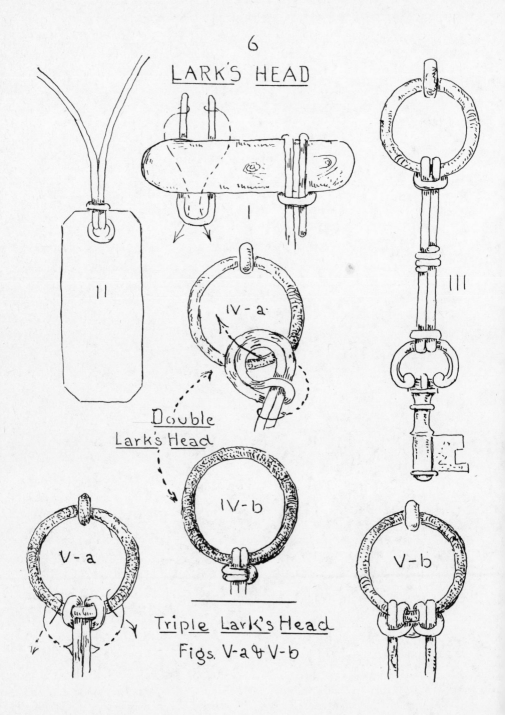

Double
Lark's Head

Triple Lark's Head
Figs. V-a & V-b

CLOVE HITCH

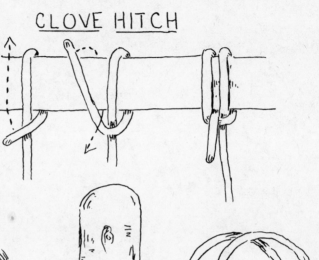

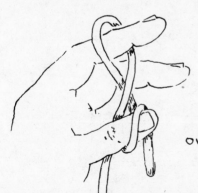

Two Half Hitches of the
same lay
over
a post

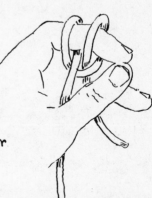

over the finger

8
CLOVE HITCH

with
Double Loop
Figs. I—III

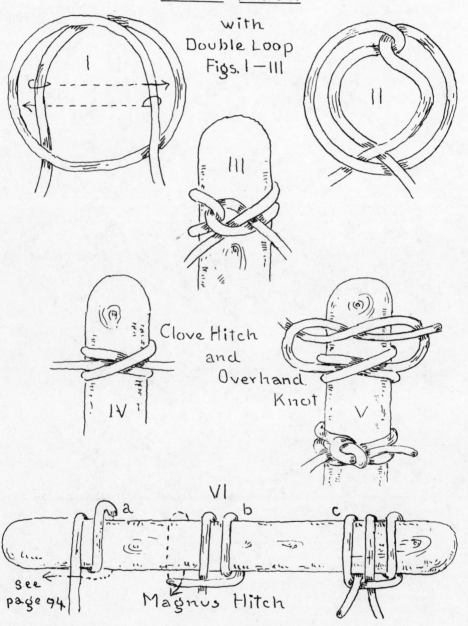

Clove Hitch
and
Overhand
Knot

VI

a   b   c

see
page 94

Magnus Hitch

OVERHAND KNOT

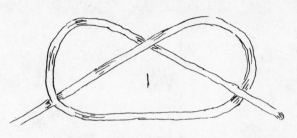

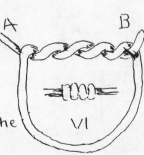

Figs. I, II
Overhand Knot
Fig. III
Overhand Noose
The knot tied with the bight of the line

Overhand
Bend

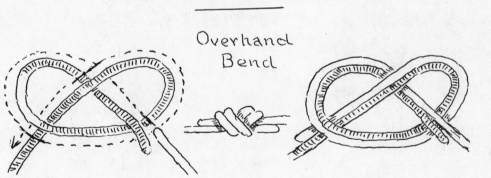

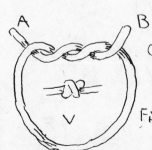

Multiple
Overhand Knots
Pull A & B sharply
Figs. V, VI
Fig. V is also known as the
Blood Knot

10
TWIN
OVERHAND KNOTS

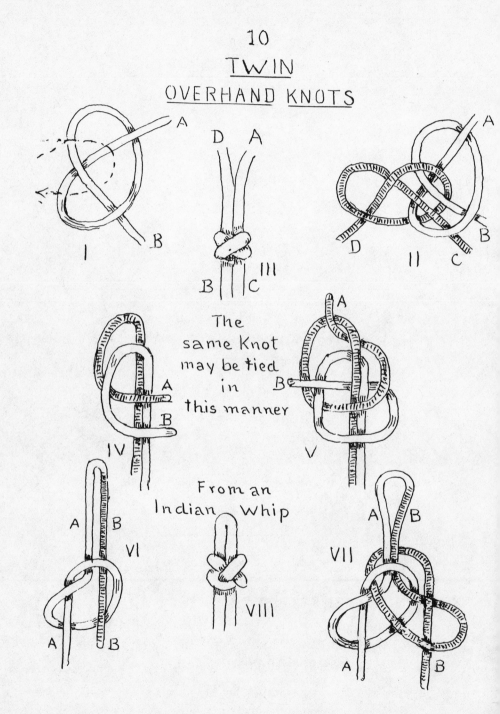

I

D A

III
B   C

A

II
D   C

B

The
same Knot
may be tied
in
this manner

IV

A
B

V

A
B

From an
Indian Whip

A   B

VI

A   B

VIII

A   B

VII

A   B

11

THE OVERHAND
KNOT

when tied with a paper
band
takes the form of
a pentagon

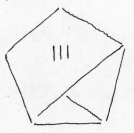

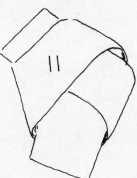

Let one end
of a length of tape
be turned over
three times
and then be pasted
onto the
other end, Fig.IV

If the tape is
cut through along
the dotted line
it becomes an endless
Overhand Knot
Fig.V.

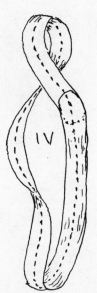

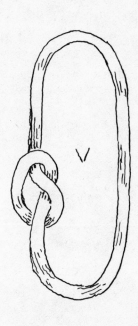

12
FIGURE OF EIGHT

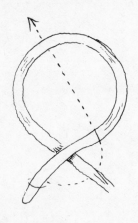

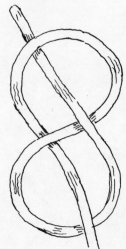

FIGURE OF EIGHT BEND

Figure of Eight and the
Miller's Knot

See page 106

Fig. of 8

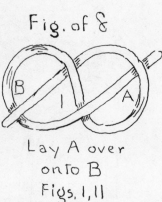

Lay A over
onto B
Figs. I, II

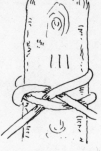

Miller's Knot

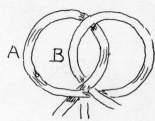

Throw the two loops
over a post
Fig III

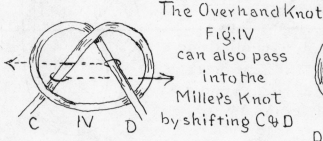

The Overhand Knot
Fig. IV
can also pass
into the
Miller's Knot
by shifting C & D

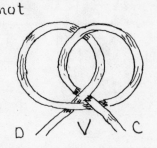

13
FIGURE of EIGHT

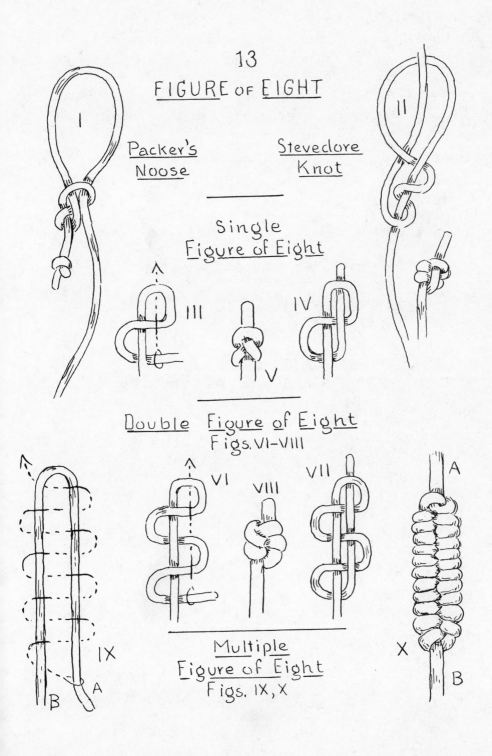

Packer's Noose

Stevedore Knot

Single Figure of Eight

I

II

III   IV

V

Double Figure of Eight
Figs. VI–VIII

VI   VIII   VII

IX

B   A

A

X

B

Multiple Figure of Eight
Figs. IX, X

ANALYSIS
of the Bends of the
forms M & N

CENTER

A One line lies on the other

B The two lines interlace

ENDS

Ends
not crossed in
the Bight

1 – Ends on same side
of the Bight

2 – Ends on different
sides of Bight

Ends
are crossed in
the Bight

3 – The Braiding is not
regular

4 – The Braiding is
regular

There are 20 possible combinations

1-A-1 1-A-2 1-A-3 1-A-4 2-A-2 2-A-3 2-A-4 3-A-3 3-A-4 4-A-4
1-B-1 1-B-2 1-B-3 1-B-4 2-B-2 2-B-3 2-B-4 3-B-3 3-B-4 4-B-4

15

Among the twenty
combinations
there are eight knots

REEF KNOT

WEAVER'S KNOT

HALF GRANNY

GRANNY

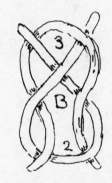

SINGLE CARRICK

HALF CARRICK

DOUBLE CARRICK (1)

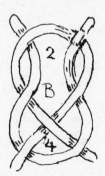

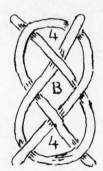

DOUBLE CARRICK (2)

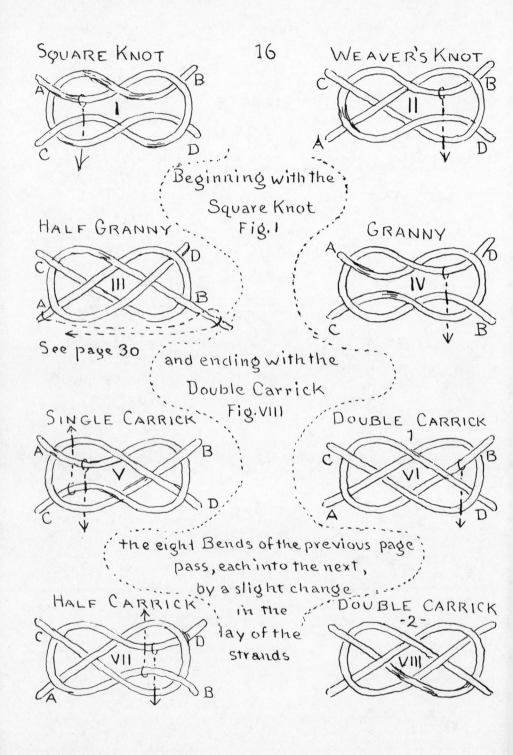

SQUARE KNOT

16

WEAVER'S KNOT

A

B

I

C

D

C

B

II

A

D

Beginning with the Square Knot Fig. I

HALF GRANNY

GRANNY

C

D

III

A

B

A

D

IV

C

B

See page 30

and ending with the Double Carrick Fig. VIII

SINGLE CARRICK

DOUBLE CARRICK

A

B

V

C

D

C

B

VI

A

D

the eight Bends of the previous page pass, each into the next, by a slight change in the lay of the strands

HALF CARRICK

DOUBLE CARRICK
-2-

C

D

VII

A

B

VIII

OBLIQUE BENDS

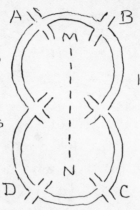

The strands
of the eight bends
are drawn
together
by pulling the ends
A and D
or
B and C

the strain
being directly
parallel
with the axis
M – N

But the strain can be applied to <u>A and C</u> or to <u>B and D</u>
in a direction oblique to the axis.
The Oblique Bends will be explained in later pages
where each is an intermediate stage
in the tying of a Loop peculiar to that Bend alone

___

The distinction between Direct and Oblique is better
presented when the Bends are tied with the ends of
a single line

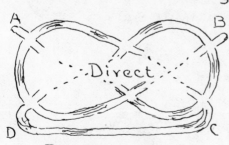

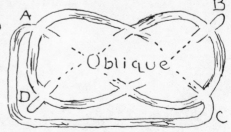

The two ends
A & B are on the same
side of the knot

The two ends
B & D are on opposite sides
of the Knot

SQUARE KNOT or REEF KNOT

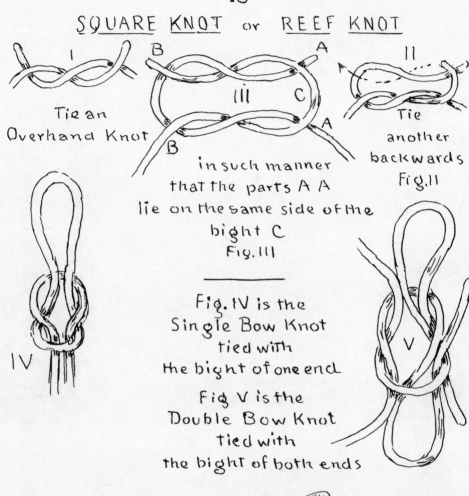

I — Tie an Overhand Knot

B ... A — in such manner that the parts A A lie on the same side of the bight C

Fig. III

II — Tie another backwards

Fig. II

Fig. IV is the Single Bow Knot tied with the bight of one end

Fig V is the Double Bow Knot tied with the bight of both ends

IV

V

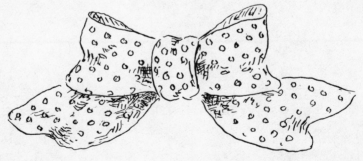

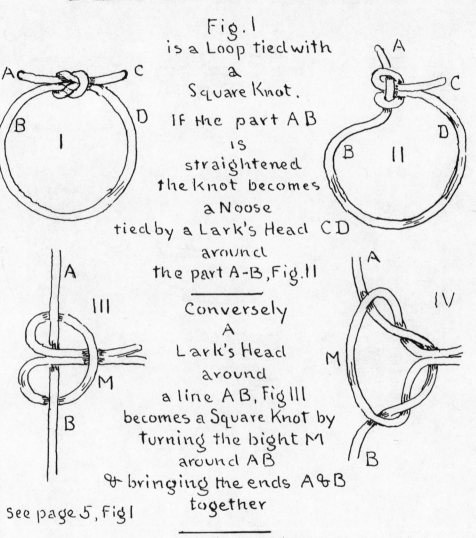

SQUARE KNOT AND LARK'S HEAD

Fig. I
is a Loop tied with
a
Square Knot.
If the part A B
is
straightened
the knot becomes
a Noose
tied by a Lark's Head CD
around
the part A-B, Fig. II

A C — C

B — I — D

A — C
B — II — D

Conversely
A
Lark's Head
around
a line AB, Fig III
becomes a Square Knot by
turning the bight M
around AB
& bringing the ends A & B
together

A
III
M
B

A
IV
M
B

See page 5, Fig I

To untie a Square Knot, straighten one of the 2 strands
Grasp the resulting Lark's Head
and strip it quickly from the straight strand

20

OBLIQUE SQUARE KNOT

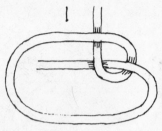

I

In Fig II pass A
to left under,
and B to right
over the strands

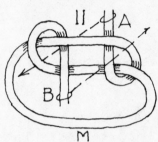

II

B

M

The Oblique
square knot
also known
as the
Thief Knot

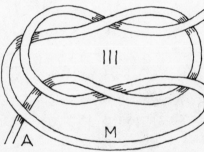

III

A

M

B

'Under strain,
however
slight,
it slips
apart.

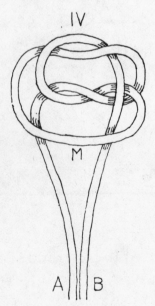

IV

M

A

B

See page 5

But
in Fig. III
bring the ends
A & B
together, Fig IV.
then with A & B
in one hand
and the part M
in the other hand
the knot becomes
a reliable
Japanese Loop.

V

M

See
page
148

MARLINE -
OR ROPE YARN KNOT

Marline is laid with
two strands

The Surgeons' Knot is a
Square Knot
of which
th first part, Fig. V-a,
is a
double Overhand Knot

The Shoe String Knot
A Bow Knot
of which
the
second part
is a
double
Overhand
Knot

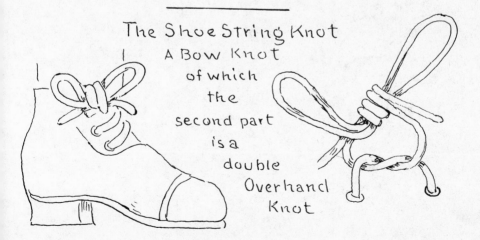

Under several names as
Weaver's Knot — Sheet Bend — Bowline & others, is
a combination of a Loop AB with
a Half Hitch CD

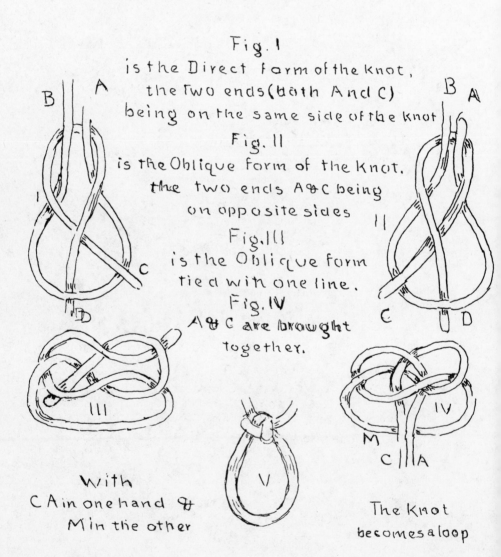

Fig. I
is the Direct form of the knot,
the two ends (both A and C)
being on the same side of the knot

Fig. II
is the Oblique form of the knot.
the two ends A & C being
on opposite sides

Fig. III
is the Oblique form
tied with one line.

Fig. IV
A & C are brought
together.

With
C A in one hand &
M in the other

The Knot
becomes a loop

23
WEAVER'S KNOT

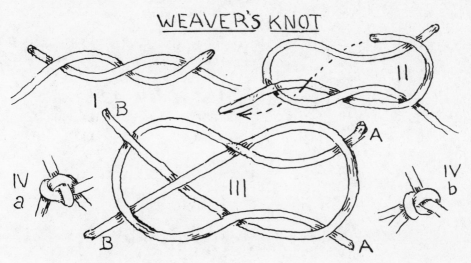

WEAVER'S KNOT
and SLIP NOOSE

Straighten the line A A Fig III
to obtain Fig. V (Crabber's Knot, p 27)

With A A pull bb until the knot
becomes a Noose
Fig. VI

Therefore
the Weaver's Knot may be tied
as follows

Tie a Noose with one line,
pass the other line through its eye
Fig. VI

Hold A A together, pull B and slip
the collar, M, up onto the loop formed by A A, Fig. VII

24
WEAVER'S KNOT

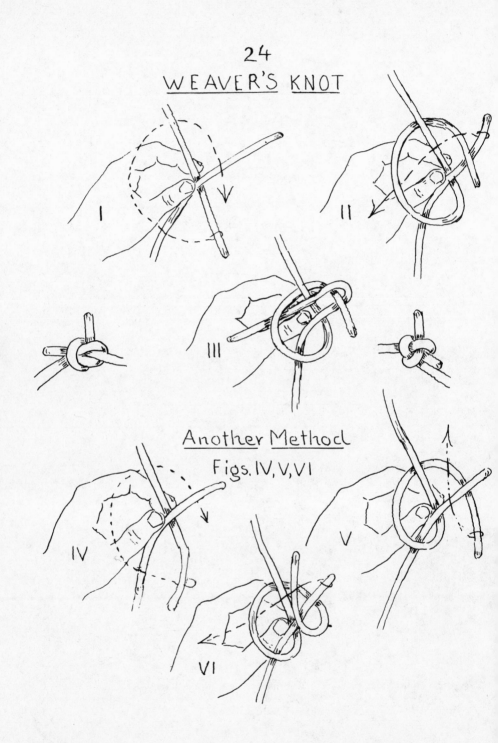

I

II

III

Another Method

Figs. IV, V, VI

IV

V

VI

The combination of a Loop with a Half Hitch
Is a reliable Knot
for joining two lines of
unequal size

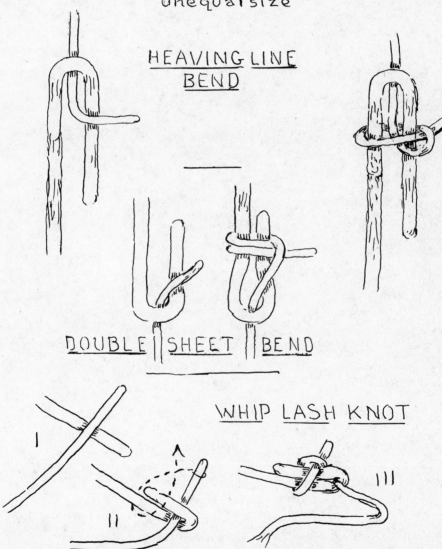

HEAVING LINE BEND

DOUBLE SHEET BEND

WHIP LASH KNOT

I

II

III

BOWLINE

Lay the end A on the standing
part B

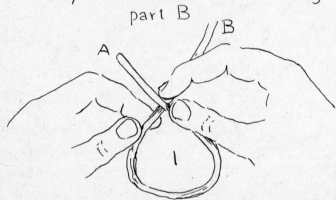

Turn the palm of the right hand up,
Forming a loop with the end A through the loop

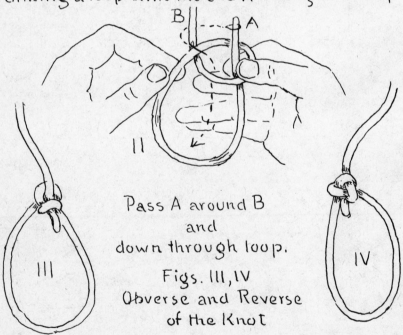

Pass A around B
and
down through loop.

Figs. III, IV
Obverse and Reverse
of the Knot

27
RUNNING BOWLINE

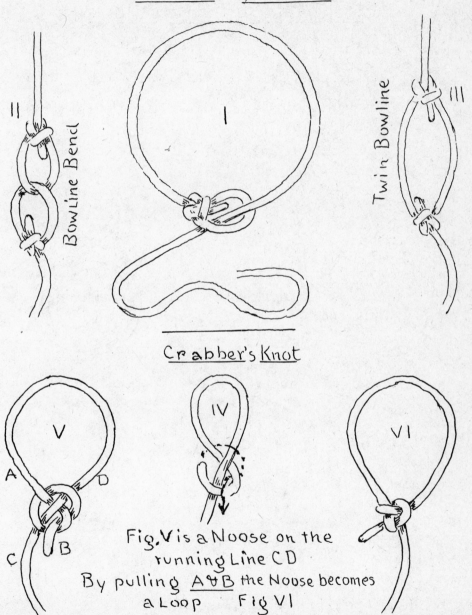

Bowline Bend

Twin Bowline

Crabber's Knot

Fig. V is a Noose on the running Line CD
By pulling A & B the Noose becomes a Loop   Fig VI

PORTUGUESE BOWLINE

Chaise de Calfat   Caulker's Chair

Fig. I - is a double Loop

Fig. II - where end A crosses the part B
tie a Bowline (III-IV)
around
the two lines

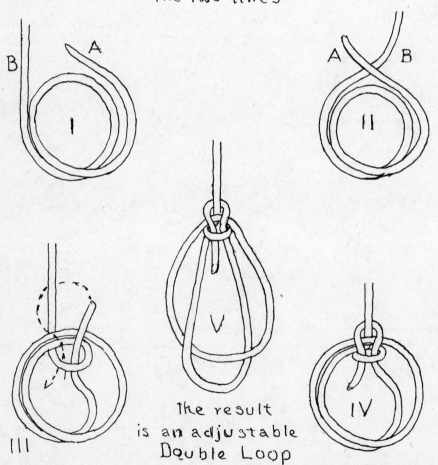

the result
is an adjustable
Double Loop

BOWLINE - ON - BIGHT

This Knot
may be tied with the bight
on any part of the line
A short length of a long rope
may be used without
cutting it

With the Loop A
tie an Overhand Knot
Fig. I

Pass the Loop A
back under the Knot
Fig. II

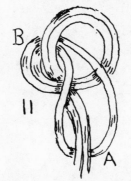

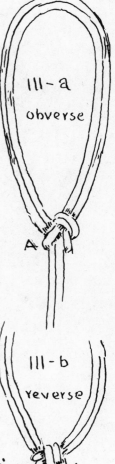

III-a
obverse

III-b
reverse

With the strands at B
Fig. II

pull the loop A into the position
shown in Figs. III-(a & b).

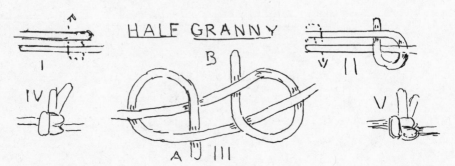

HALF GRANNY

This knot, when pulled taut, is peculiar
Figs. IV, V
The two ends lie side by side
The two faces; both obverse and reverse,
are alike.

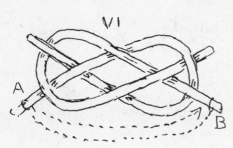

Fig. VI
is the form of the knot
shown on pages 15-16.
When pulled taut,
it takes the form shown
in Fig. IV (or V)

In Fig. VI interchange A & B
to form VII
In Fig. VII turn the right
hand half of the knot
over to form Fig. VIII
(or Fig. III above)
III, VI & VII, when taut are
alike and are forms of the
HALF GRANNY

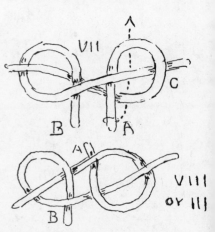

THE GRASS KNOT

is the Half Granny as a
bend for straps, straw,
grass or
such flat material

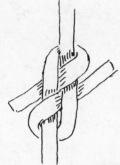

II

THE REEVING LINE BEND

III

is a form of the Half Granny

NOTE

IV

B   A

A   V

B

C

VII

D

In the Half Granny
Fig. IV
by interchanging
the ends A & B
the knot passes into
the Oblique Granny
Fig. V
The Half Granny must not
be confused with Fig. VI,
which slips and which,
by interchanging
C and D,
passes into the
Thief (Oblique Reef) Knot Fig. VII

VI

D   C

THE GRANNY

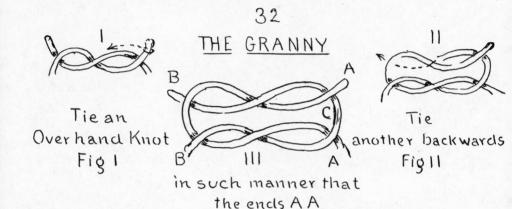

Tie an Overhand Knot
Fig I

Tie another backwards
Fig II

in such manner that
the ends A A
lie on opposite sides of the bight C

GRANNY
and
CLOVE HITCH

See page 5, Fig II

Straighten
the line A A, Fig III
The parts BB-C become a
Clove Hitch
around the line A A

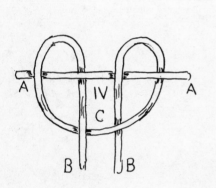

A Granny, therefore, may be tied as follows.

Tie a
Clove Hitch
around the line
A A
Fig. IV

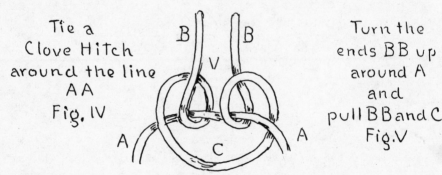

Turn the
ends BB up
around A
and
pull BB and C
Fig. V

OBLIQUE GRANNY

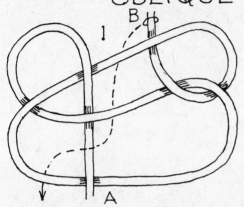

Fig I is the Half Granny.
Pass the end B down
under two strands and
over the strand A.
The knot becomes
Fig II
The Oblique Granny

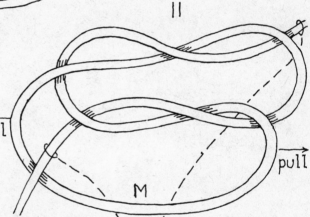

When this knot
is pulled taut,
it slips apart
and will not
hold.

But, by bringing the ends
A & B together Fig. II,
by holding A & B in one
hand and the part M
in the other, Fig II
becomes a reliable Loop.

See page 5

The Japanese method of tying
this Loop is shown on page 148.

BUNTLINE HITCH AND OBLIQUE GRANNY

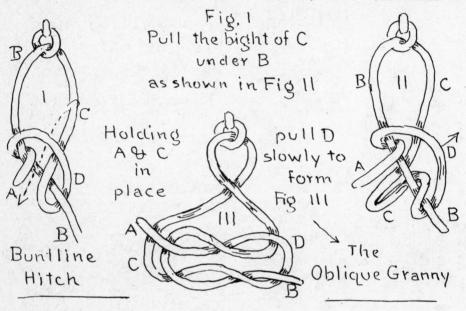

Fig. 1
Pull the bight of C
under B
as shown in Fig II

B   II   C

Holding
A & C
in
place

pull D
slowly to
form
Fig III

III

B

Buntline
Hitch

The
Oblique Granny

FOUR-
IN-HAND
TIE

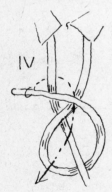

IV

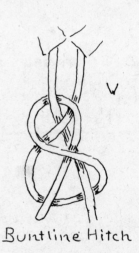

V

Buntline Hitch

35

SINGLE CARRICK BEND

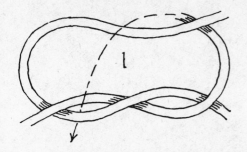 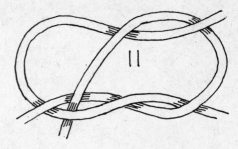

The two bights that form
the finished knot, lie on
planes perpendicular to
each other.
The lay of the strands
resembles that of the
four strand Round Braid.

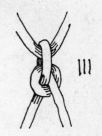

Single Carrick

Fig. IV
Single Carrick
and Fig. V
Half Carrick
are very much alike.
They differ in the
braiding of their
strands,
alternately
over and under
in Fig V
very irregular
in Fig IV

Half Carrick

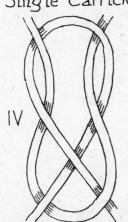

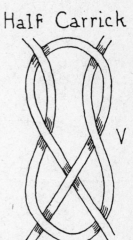

36
DOUBLE CARRICK
No. 1

This Knot
differs from
the Double Carrick No 2
by the
irregular braiding
of the strands

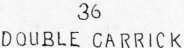

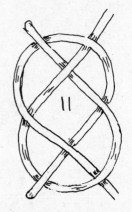

III

Fig. V begins with an
Overhand Knot Fig. IV

Fig. VII begins with the
Miller's Knot Fig. VI

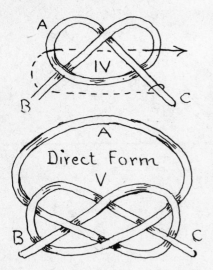

A
IV
B
C

A
Direct Form
V
B
C

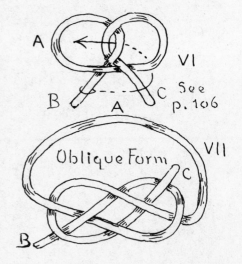

A
B
C
VI
See p. 106
A

Oblique Form
VII
C
B

HALF CARRICK

This is Nameless-2 of the first edition

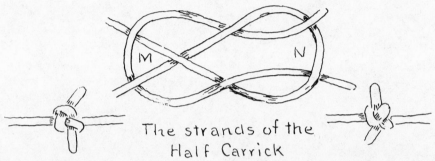

The strands of the
Half Carrick
in one half (M) of the knot, have the lay characteristic
of the Double Carrick-No. 2.
The strands of the other half (N) correspond with the
lay of the Granny.

So far as I know
this knot
is not in use

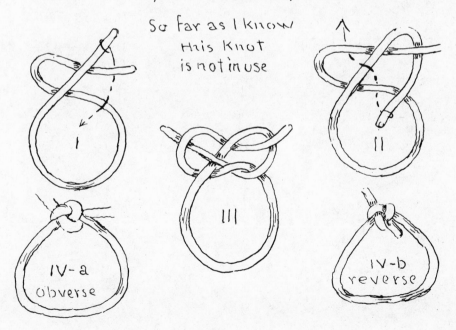

OBLIQUE HALF CARRICK

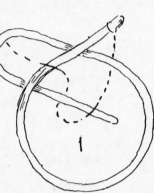

In Fig II
bring the ends
A & B
together

Fig III
Hold A & B
in one hand and
pull M

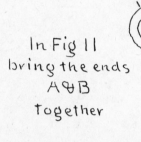

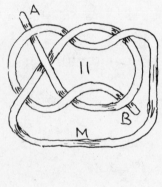

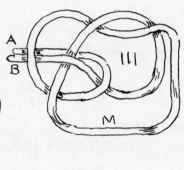

HALF CARRICK and MILLER'S KNOT

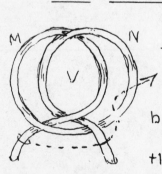

Fig. V,
the Miller's Knot
(pages 12, 106)
can pass
by a slight change
into Fig. VI,
the Half Carrick

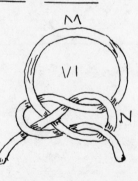

DOUBLE CARRICK
No. 2

This knot
differs from the
Double Carrick No 1
by the
regular braiding
of its strands

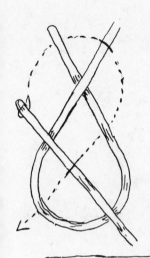

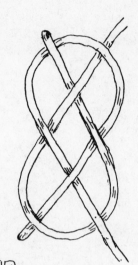

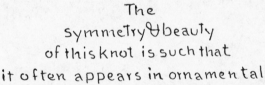

The
symmetry & beauty
of this knot is such that
it often appears in ornamental
combinations

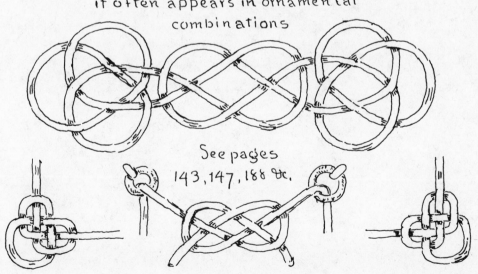

See pages
143, 147, 188 &c.

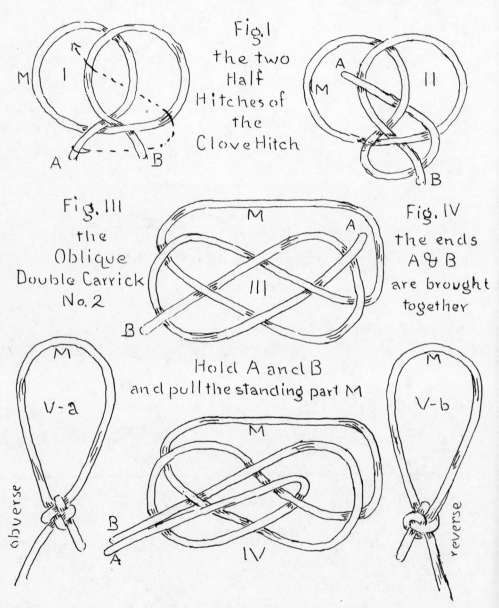

40)

OBLIQUE DOUBLE CARRICK
No. 2

Fig. I
the two
Half
Hitches of
the
Clove Hitch

M   I

A   B

M   A   II

B

Fig. III
the
Oblique
Double Carrick
No. 2

M   A
III
B

Fig. IV
the ends
A & B
are brought
together

M
V-a

obverse

Hold A and B
and pull the standing part M

M

B
A   IV

M
V-b

reverse

NOOSE

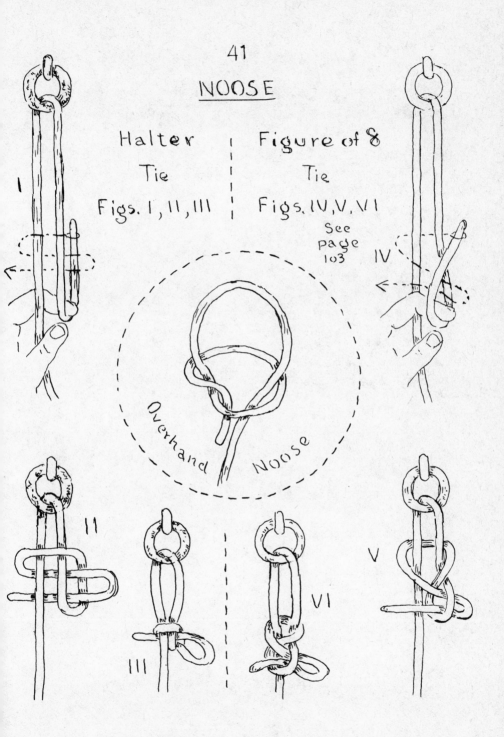

Halter Tie
Figs. I, II, III

Figure of 8 Tie
Figs. IV, V, VI
See page 103

Overhand Noose

I

IV

II

III

VI

V

DOUBLE NOOSE

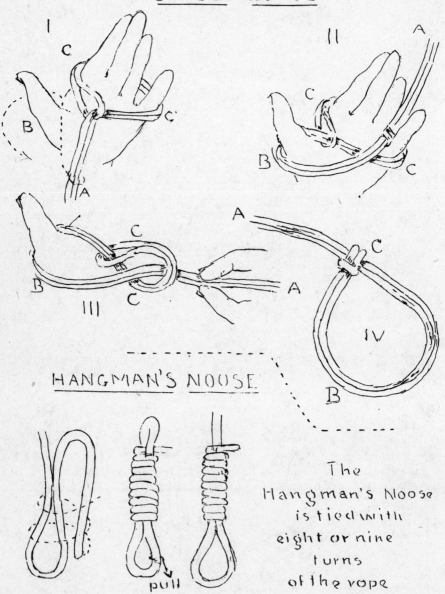

HANGMAN'S NOOSE

pull

The
Hangman's Noose
is tied with
eight or nine
turns
of the rope

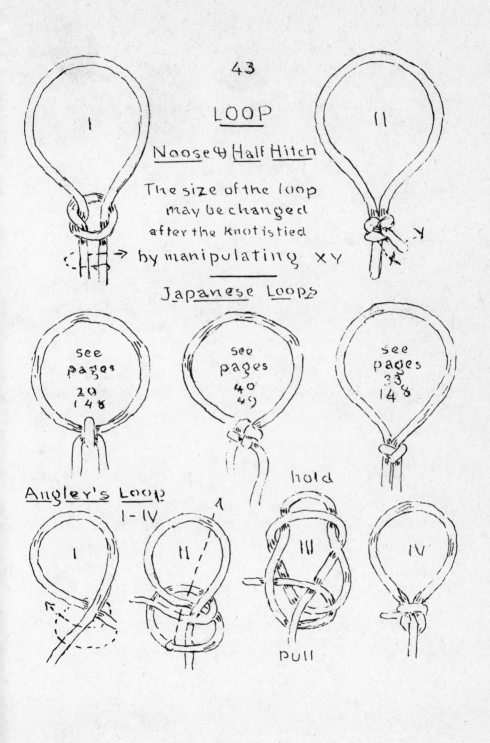

LOOP

Noose & Half Hitch

The size of the loop
may be changed
after the knot is tied
→ by manipulating XY

Japanese Loops

see
pages
20
148

see
pages
40
49

see
pages
33
148

Angler's Loop I-IV

I

II

hold

III

pull

IV

44
ARTILLERY
or
MAN - HARNESS
KNOT

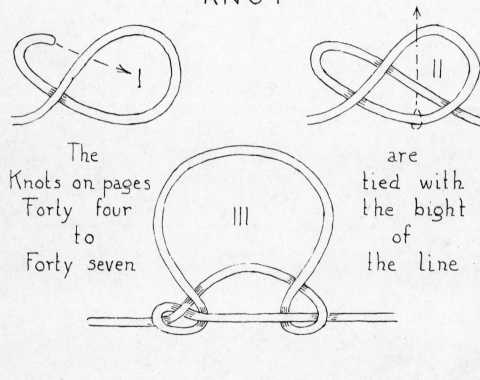

The
Knots on pages
Forty four
to
Forty seven

are
tied with
the bight
of
the line

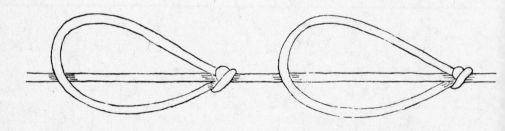

LINEMAN'S KNOT

LOOP

beginning with an Overhand Knot

Fig. 1

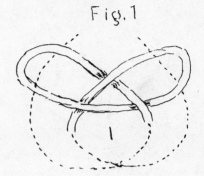

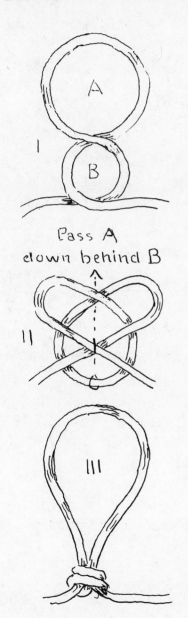

I

Pass A
down behind B

II

III

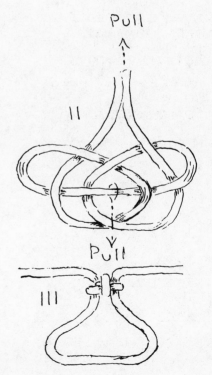

Pull

II

Pull

III

46
DOUBLE LOOP

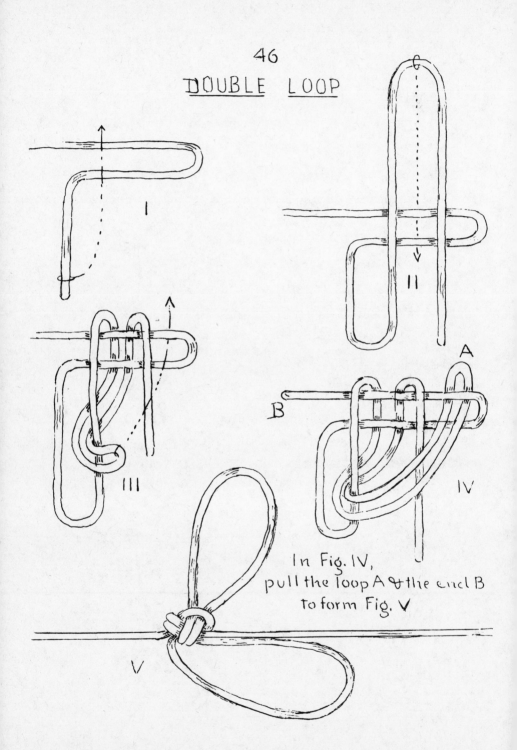

I

II

III

IV

A

B

C

In Fig. IV,
pull the loop A & the end B
to form Fig. V

V

DOUBLE LOOPS

SPANISH BOWLINE

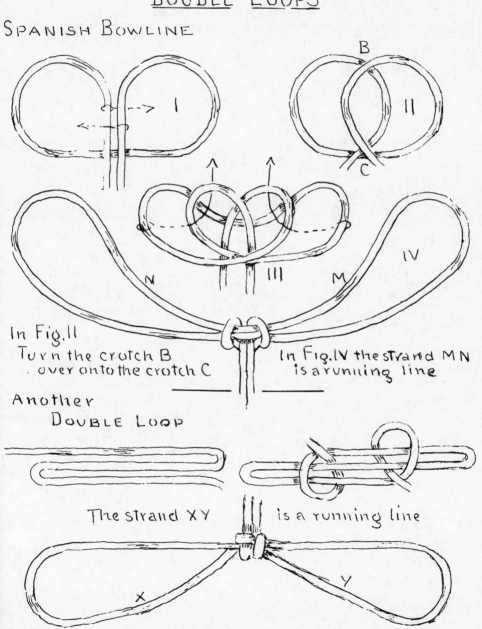

In Fig.II
Turn the crotch B
over onto the crotch C

In Fig.IV the strand MN
is a running line

Another
DOUBLE LOOP

The strand XY   is a running line

STOPPER KNOTS

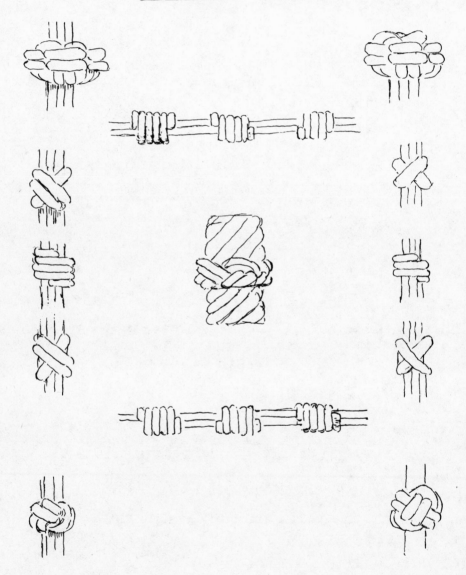

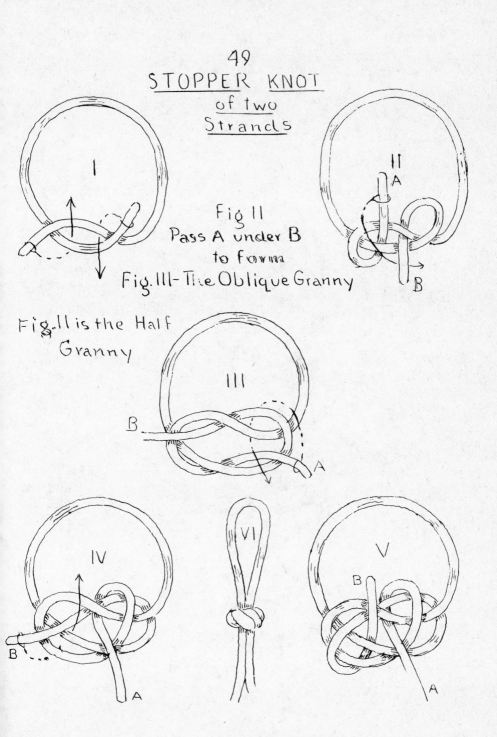

49
STOPPER KNOT
of two
Strands

I

Fig II
Pass A under B
to Form
Fig. III - The Oblique Granny

Fig. II is the Half
Granny

II

A

B

III

B

A

IV

B

A

VI

V

B

A

WALL KNOT

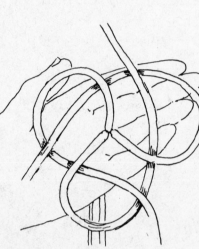

With 3 cords
the wall may be
tied
to the right
or
to the left

With a
rope
the wall must
follow
the lay of the
strands

CROWN KNOT

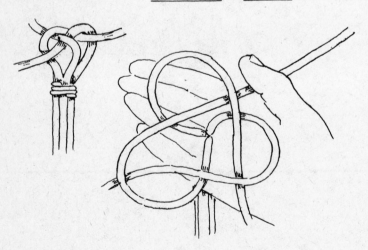

MAN - ROPE
KNOT

A
combination
of the
Wall & Crown
with the strands doubled

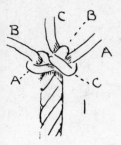

Single Wall

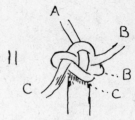

II Single
Wall & Crown

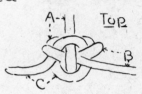

In doubling
each strand follows
its own lay

V

The Crown
Fig. II
brings each end
against
its own part

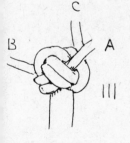

III

Double Wall
&
Single Crown

The 3 ends A B C
Fig III
are passed down
through the center of
the knot
Fig. IV
and are cut off

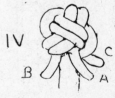

IV

Double
Wall & Crown

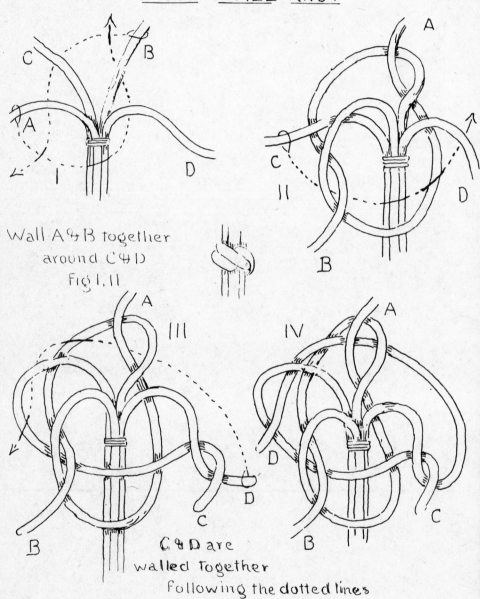

52

TWIN WALL KNOT

C   B

A

D

I

Wall A & B together
around C & D
Fig I, II

A

C

D

II

B

III

A

B

D

C

C & D are
walled together
following the dotted lines

IV

A

D

B

C

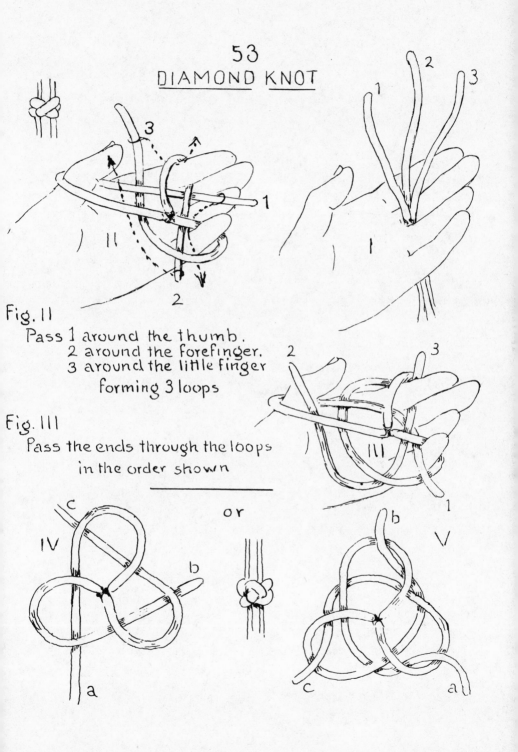

53
DIAMOND KNOT

3

1

II

2

1 **2** **3**

I

2 **3**

III

1

Fig. II
Pass 1 around the thumb.
2 around the forefinger.
3 around the little finger

forming 3 loops

Fig. III
Pass the ends through the loops
in the order shown

---

c

IV

b

a

or

b

V

c **a**

54
DIAMOND KNOT
of
Four
Strands

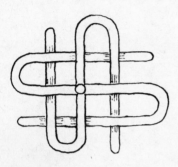

III

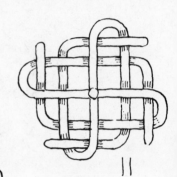

II

DIAMOND
of
Two   Strands

Fig IV
The
Oblique
Double Carrick
No 2
See page 40
Fig III

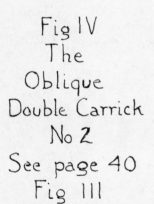

IV

VII

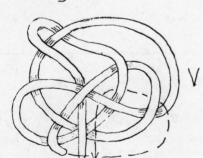

V

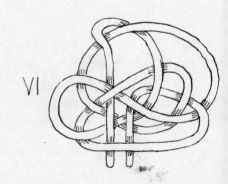

VI

55
DOUBLE DIAMOND

Fig I is the
Diamond Knot

In doubling
each strand follows
its own lay

For practise with this, and with the various
Stopper Knots.
the construction is more easily followed if the strands
are of different colors.

First stage.

In Fig. I
{ pass A over C & under B
pass B over A & under C
pass C over B & under A
to form Fig II

Second stage

In Fig. II
{ pass A over both strands of C & under both strands of B
pass B over both strands of A & under both strands of C
pass C over both strands of B & under both strands of A

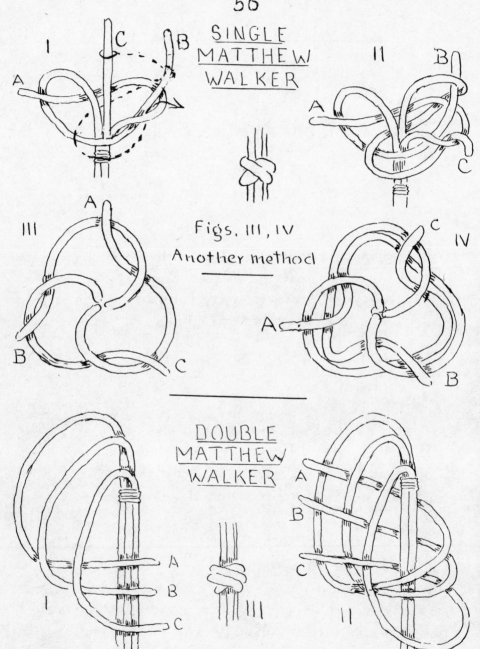

56

SINGLE
MATTHEW
WALKER

I C B

A

II B

A

C

Figs. III, IV
Another method

III A

B C

IV C

A

B

DOUBLE
MATTHEW
WALKER

I

III

II A

B

C

INVERTED WALL KNOT

Button of 3 Strands

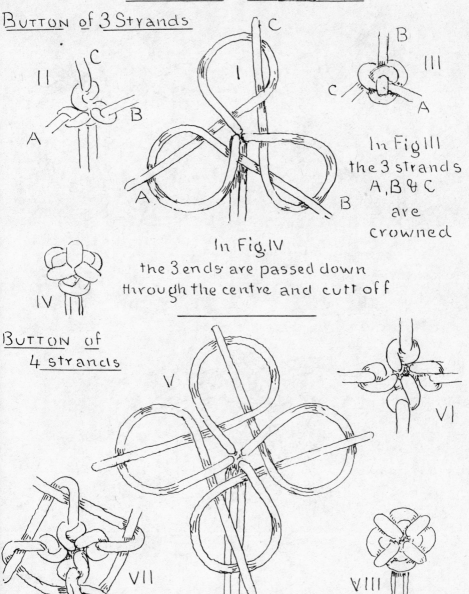

II C B A

I C

III B C A

In Fig III
the 3 strands
A,B & C
are
crowned

In Fig. IV
the 3 ends are passed down
through the centre and cutt off

IV

Button of
4 strands

V

VI

VII

VIII

STAR KNOT

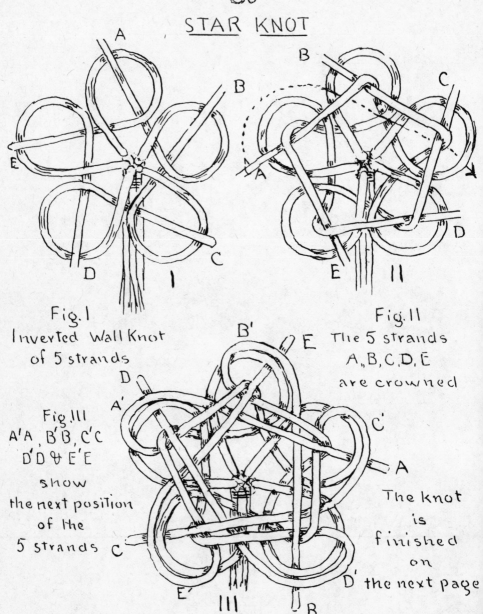

Fig. I
Inverted Wall Knot
of 5 strands

Fig. II
The 5 strands
A, B, C, D, E
are crowned

Fig. III
A'A, B'B, C'C
D'D & E'E
show
the next position
of the
5 strands

The knot
is
finished
on
the next page

STAR KNOT
Continued

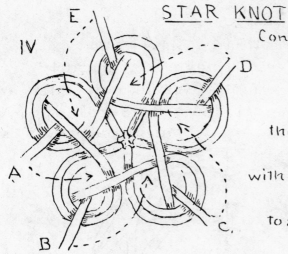

IV

E

D

A

B

C

Fig IV

is

the reverse side of

Fig. III

with some of the strands

omitted

to avoid confusion

Fig V

(reverse side)

The ends A, B, C, D and E

following the arrows in Fig IV

pass up through

the bights and the center of the

knot

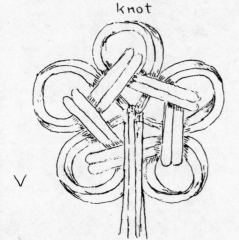

V

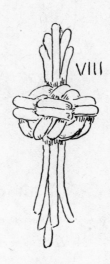

VI

VIII

TURK'S HEAD

A Turk's Head may be defined
as a complex of like interlacing circles
so united as to form a single line, and whose centers are
the angles of a regular polygon of 3, 4, 5 or of any conve-
-nient number of sides.

This diagram shows 3 forms of Turk's Head with the same heptagonal center.

The lines AO, BO, CO, divide the figure into three sections

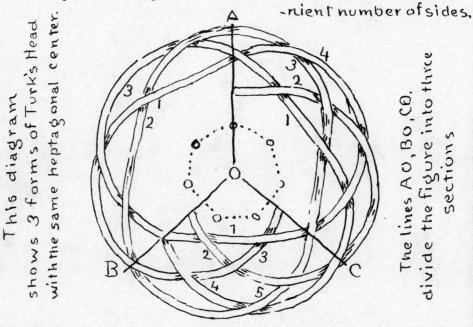

The section AOB
represents a heptagonal Turk's Head of three strands

the section AOC
of 4 strands

the section BOC
of 5 strands

TURK'S HEAD
Triangular Center
Two strands

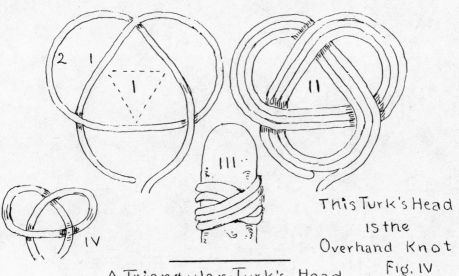

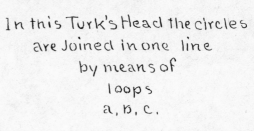

This Turk's Head
is the
Overhand Knot
Fig. IV

A Triangular Turk's Head
with 4 Strands

In this Turk's Head the circles
are joined in one line
by means of
loops
a, b, c.

On account of the crowded
interlacing
at the center of the knot
this method is not practicable
for centers of four or more sides

62

TURK'S HEAD

Quadrangular Center

Three strands

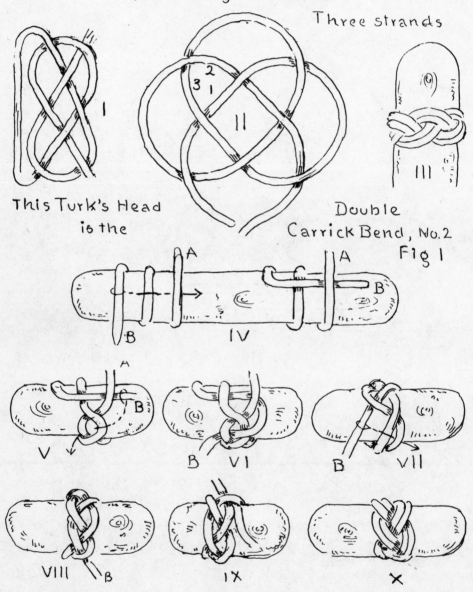

This Turk's Head is the

Double Carrick Bend, No. 2

Fig I

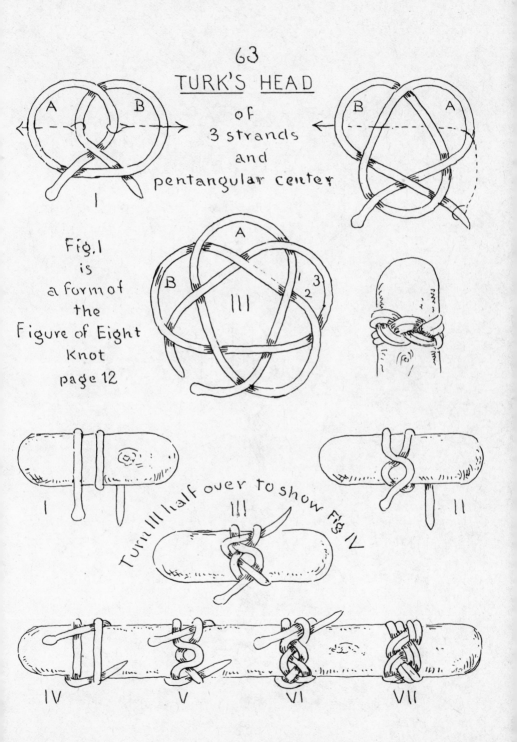

63
TURK'S HEAD
of
3 strands
and
pentangular center

A   B

I

B   A

Fig. 1
is
a form of
the
Figure of Eight
Knot
page 12

A

B   1 3
2

III

I

Turn III half over to show Fig. IV

III

II

IV   V   VI   VII

TURK'S HEAD

pentagonal,
of
three strands,
tied on the
hand

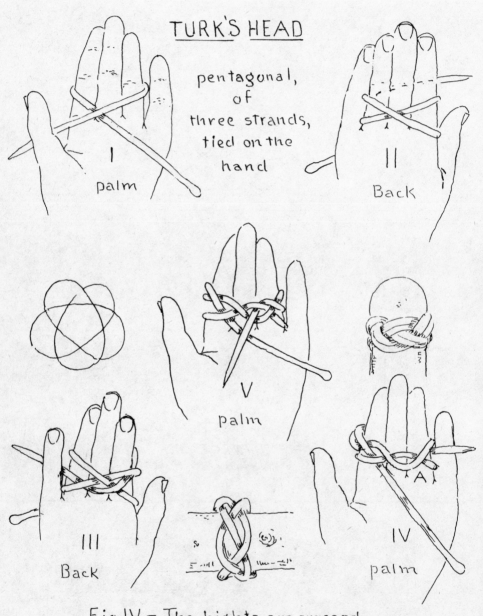

I palm

II Back

III Back

IV palm

V palm

Fig IV – The bights are crossed
at A

65

TURK'S HEAD
of
four strands
and pentangular center

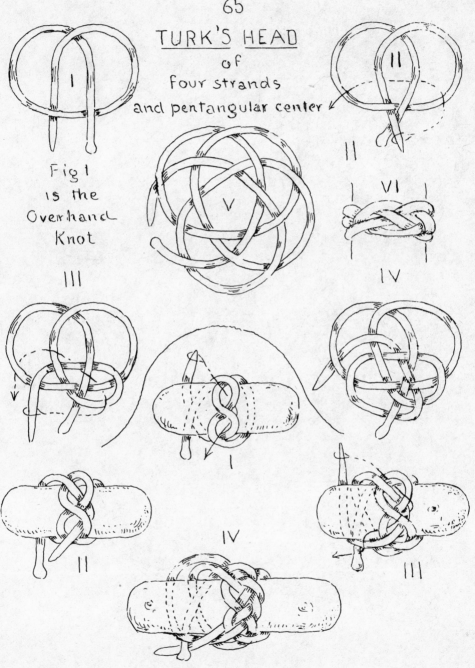

Fig 1
is the
Overhand
Knot

66

TURK'S HEAD
as a
Stopper
Knot

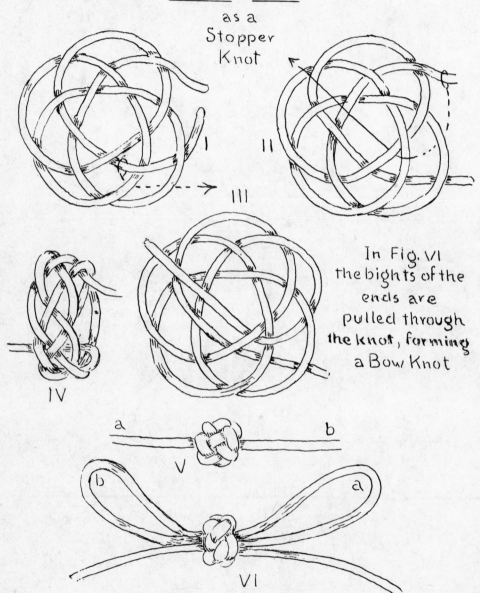

In Fig. VI
the bights of the
ends are
pulled through
the knot, forming
a Bow Knot

67
TURK'S HEAD
as a
BUTTON

I

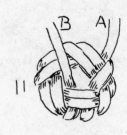

B   A

II

Fig. I - Turk's Head

B

III   A

Fig. II - The strands
are double

Fig. III
End A carried down through
the Knot

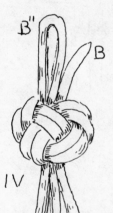

B"

B

IV

B'   A

top of knot

V

Fig. V
A and B' are crowned
and are passed up through
the centre of the crown
coming out
alongside of B-B"
All ends are cut off except
one loop
Fig. VI

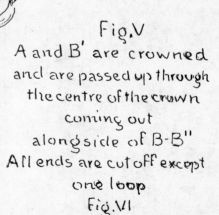

VI

Fig. IV
End B is carried down
and back through
the Knot
forming two loops
B' and B"

68

SENNIT

Plaiting with an uneven number of strands

I

II

The outer strands
in alternate order
pass over
2 strands, Fig 1,
3 strands, Fig 2,
(or any convenient number)
meeting in a
"herring-bone" central line

FRENCH SENNIT

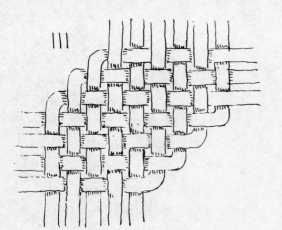

III

The strands
in
this method
may be
odd or even
in number

69
SENNIT

Of Five Strands

Of Seven Strands

Of Nine Strands

SENNIT

of three Strands

Forming

a

Ring

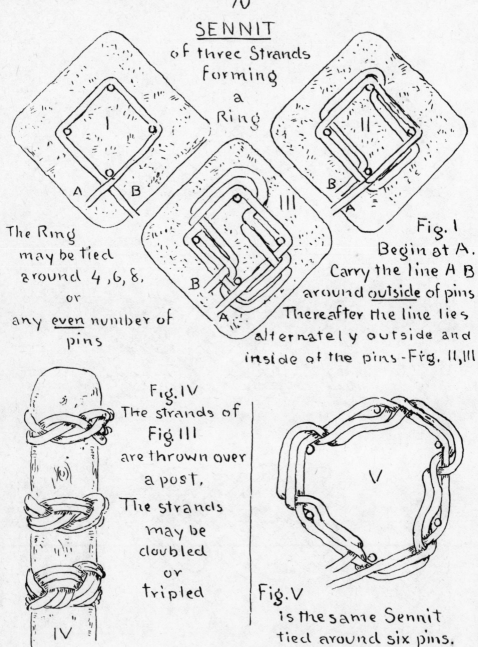

The Ring
may be tied
around 4, 6, 8,
or
any *even* number of
pins

Fig. 1
Begin at A.
Carry the line A B
around *outside* of pins
Thereafter the line lies
alternately outside and
inside of the pins - Frg. II, III

Fig. IV
The strands of
Fig III
are thrown over
a post,
The strands
may be
doubled
or
tripled

Fig. V
is the same Sennit
tied around six pins.

SENNIT

of Five and Seven Strands forming Rings
In addition to the four fixed pins, others are needed to
hold the work
in place

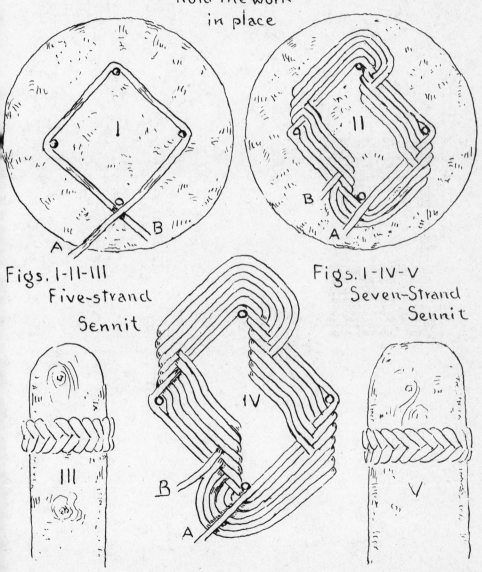

Figs. I-II-III
Five-strand
Sennit

Figs. I-IV-V
Seven-Strand
Sennit

THREE-STRAND SENNTS
tied with one line

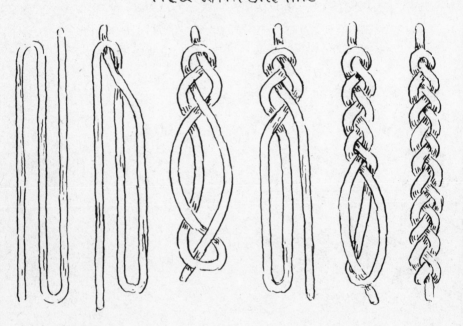

Overhand Knot

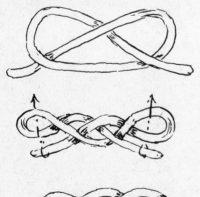

Figure of Eight Knot

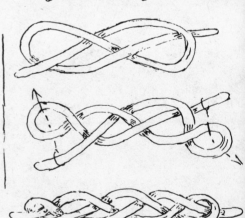

TRIANGULAR BRAID OF TWO STRANDS

Fig. I A loop C is formed by tying an Overhand Knot with the bight of strand A

Fig II With the fingers through the loop C seize B, pull it through the loop C, at the same time pull A thus forming a new Loop D

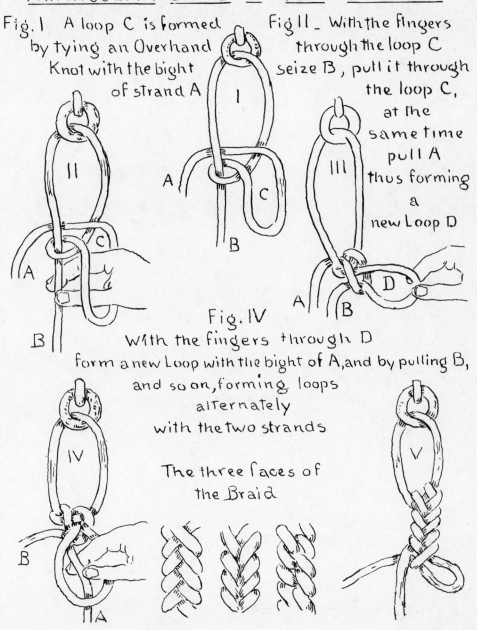

Fig. IV
With the fingers through D form a new Loop with the bight of A, and by pulling B, and so on, forming loops alternately with the two strands

The three faces of the Braid

SINGLE STRAND SQUARE BRAID

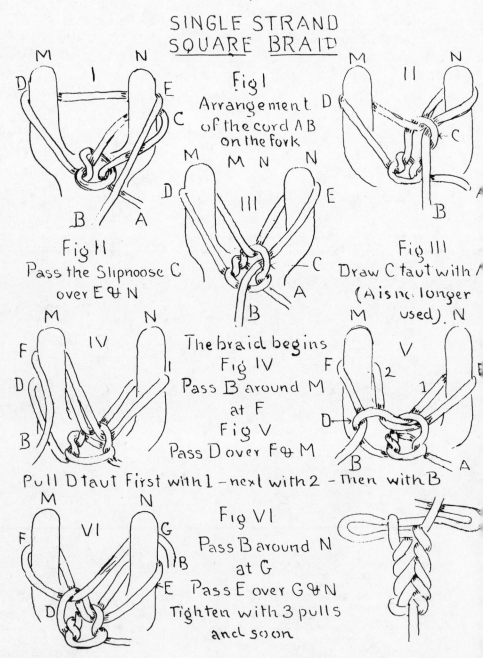

Fig I
Arrangement of the cord A B on the fork

Fig II
Pass the Slipnoose C over E & N

Fig III
Draw C taut with A (A is no longer used). N

The braid begins
Fig IV
Pass B around M at F
Fig V
Pass D over F & M

Pull D taut First with 1 — next with 2 — Then with B

Fig VI
Pass B around N at G
Pass E over G & N
Tighten with 3 pulls
and so on

75

BRAID
OF THREE STRANDS

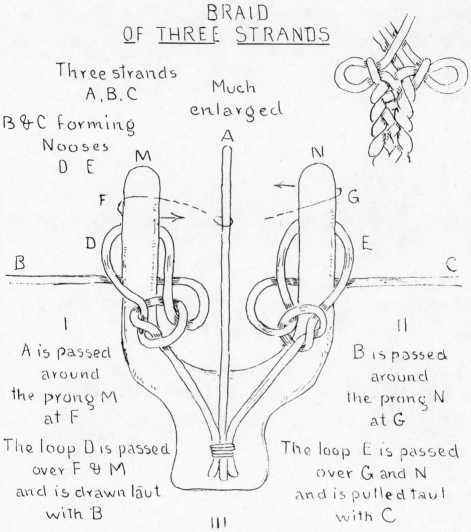

Three strands
A, B, C

B & C forming
Nooses
D E

Much
enlarged

A

M

N

F

G

D

E

B

C

I

II

A is passed
around
the prong M
at F

B is passed
around
the prong N
at G

The loop D is passed
over F & M
and is drawn laut
with B

The loop E is passed
over G and N
and is pulled taut
with C

III

C is then passed around M etc.

The strand that pulls its loop taut forms the next
new loop

The arrows at F & G indicate the lay of the
strands that form the new loops.

FOUR-STRAND ROUND BRAID

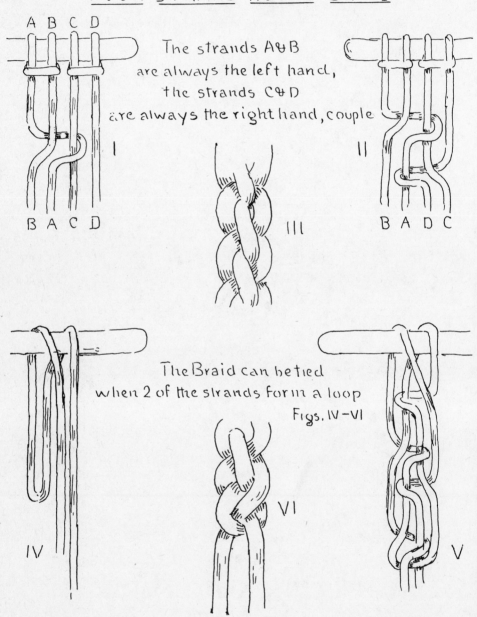

The strands A & B
are always the left hand,
the strands C & D
are always the right hand, couple

The Braid can be tied
when 2 of the strands form a loop
Figs. IV–VI

ROUND BRAID

tied with a doubled strand

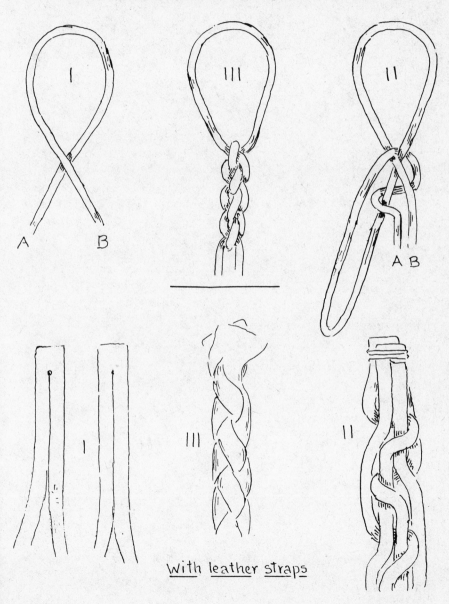

I

III

II

A   B

A B

With leather straps

I   III   II

FOUR-STRAND FLAT BRAID

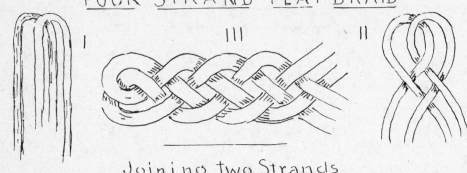

I   III   II

Joining two Strands
A and B

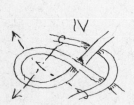

Figs. IV, V
the
Carrick Bend B

The Braid can be extended indefinitely at each
end or at both ends Figs. VI, VII, VIII

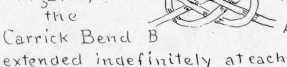

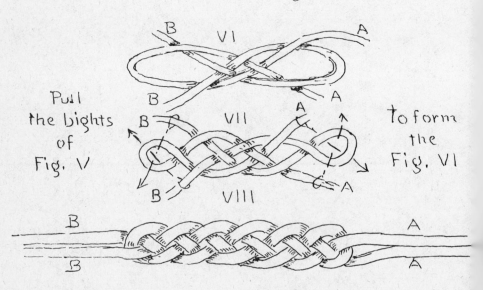

VI

Pull
the bights
of
Fig. V

B   VII   A

To form
the
Fig. VI

VIII

B
B   A
A

A SIX-STRAND AND EIGHT-STRAND BRAID

Half Round Braid

Front

Back

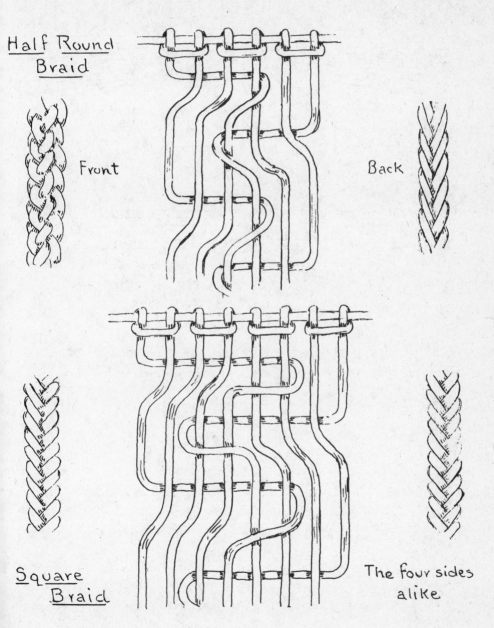

Square Braid

The four sides alike

SQUARE BRAID

of ten strands

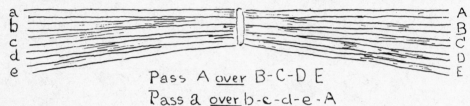

Pass A over B-C-D-E
Pass a over b-c-d-e-A
Pass b under c-d-e-A   Pass B under C-D-E-a-b

I

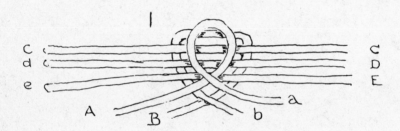

Pass C over D-E-a-b   Pass c over d-e-A-B-C
Pass d under e-A-B-C   Pass D under E-a-b-c-d

II

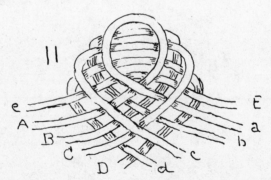

Fig. II repeats the method of Fig. I
and its repetition forms the Braid.

CROWN BRAID

This is the Crown Knot
repeated in superposed layers

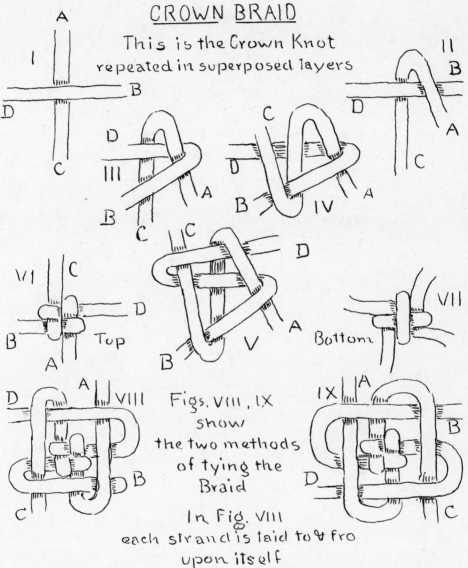

Figs. VIII, IX
show
the two methods
of tying the
Braid

In Fig. VIII
each strand is laid to & fro
upon itself
reversing, in the alternate layers, the order of rotation
In Fig. IX
the order of rotation is always the same

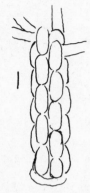

CROWN BRAID

Fig. I

is the Braid tied by the method of
Fig. VIII on the last page

Fig. II

is the Braid tied by the method of
Fig. IX, on the last page

Six-Strand Braid

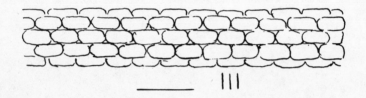

III

The Braid may be tied around
a Core, Fig. IV

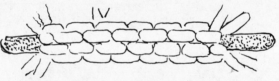

IV

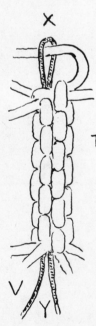

The Core may be pulled out
Fig. V

and, with a copper wire X-Y,
the strands
at each end of the Braid
can be drawn
through the centre, Fig. VI, so as
to form
a neat finish at both ends

83

CHAIN BRAID

Single   Double

tied with the   tied with the
Bight   End
A   B

The
single
Chain Braid
is the fundamental knot
in Crochet & Knitting

84

FALSE BRAID
in
Leather

I

III

II

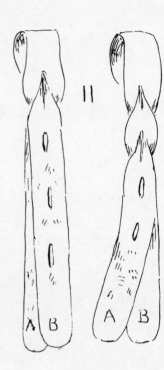

A   B

A   B

A   B

Splicing 2 straps

Strap & Buckle

The leather straps
while wet
are pulled in alternate order
through
the slots

85
FALSE BRAID

Three straps may unite in a False Braid
as shown in Fig I

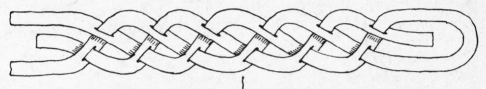

I

Four straps may also be combined as
shown in Fig II

II

The slits are cut one by one as the work progresses

The Braid will be square in cross section
when, with 2 straps, the width of the strap is twice
its thickness—with 3 straps, 3 times, & with
4 straps, 4 times the thickness.

The 3 methods may combine to form a Leash or Quirt

III

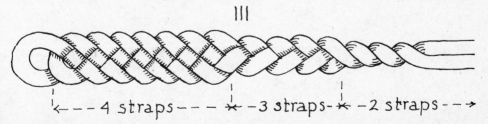

←- - 4 straps - - - ✶ - 3 straps- ✶ - 2 straps - - →

86

TRICK BRAID

Fig. I – Leather strap with two slits and three strands

Fig. II – A over B and C over A

Pass M through X

to form Fig. III

Fig IV

B over C, A over B

M through Y.

Repeat

as desired

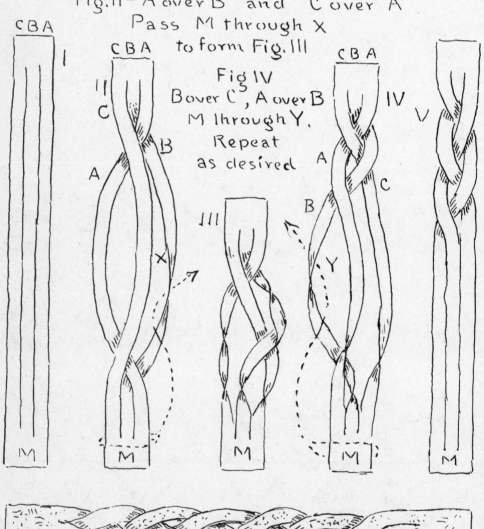

CBA

I

CBA

II

C

B

A

III

M

M

CBA

IV

V

A

C

B

Y

M

M

VI

SAILORS KNOTS
REEVING
LINE

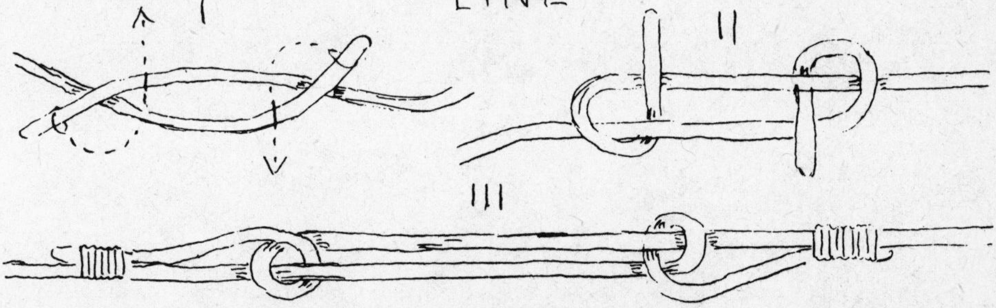

I

II

III

Fig. II is the Half Granny   see page 30

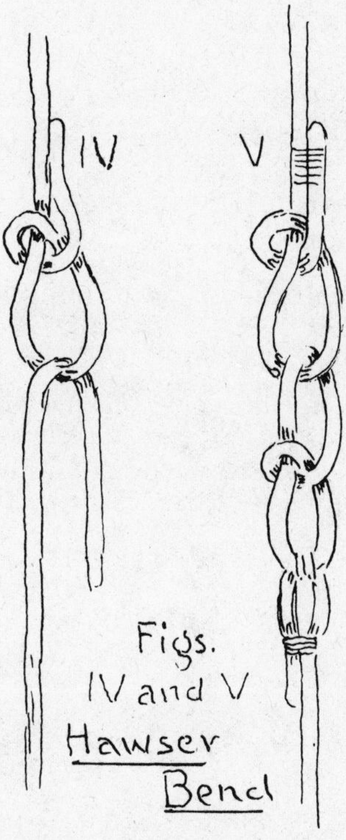

IV   V

Temporary
Bend

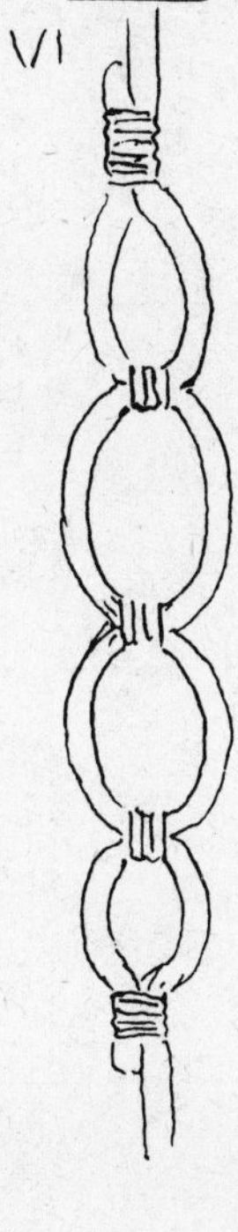

VI

Spanish
Hawser
Bend

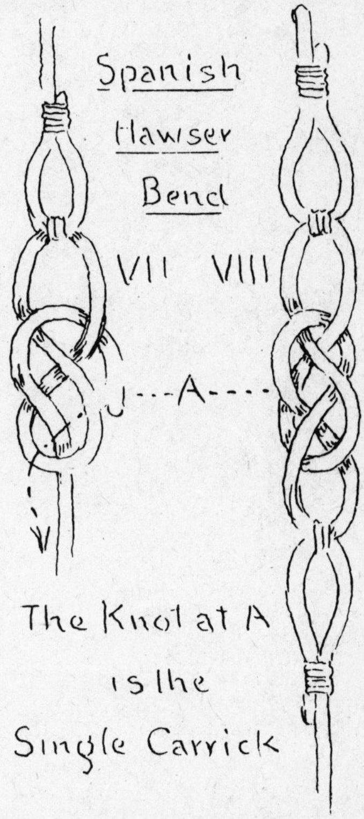

VII   VIII

J....A....

Figs.
IV and V
Hawser
Bend

The Knot at A
is the
Single Carrick

88
HITCHES

Hook and Half Hitch

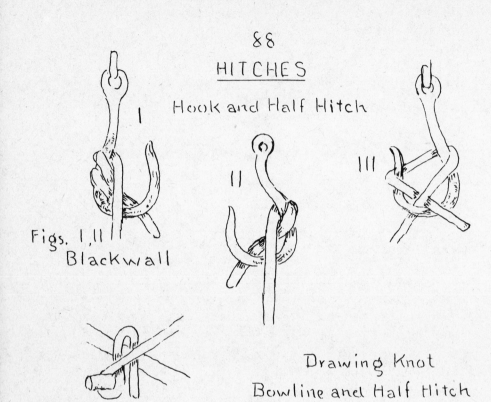

Figs. I, II
Blackwall

I

II

III

Slippery Hitch

Drawing Knot
Bowline and Half Hitch

Backhanded Hitch

I----II

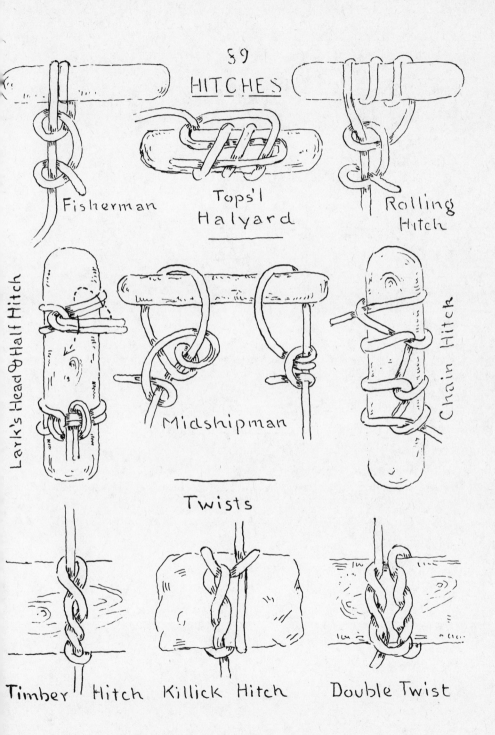

§9

HITCHES

Fisherman

Tops'l Halyard

Rolling Hitch

Lark's Head & Half Hitch

Midshipman

Chain Hitch

Twists

Timber Hitch

Killick Hitch

Double Twist

CATSPAW

Single

I

Form two
Loops
as
in Fig. I

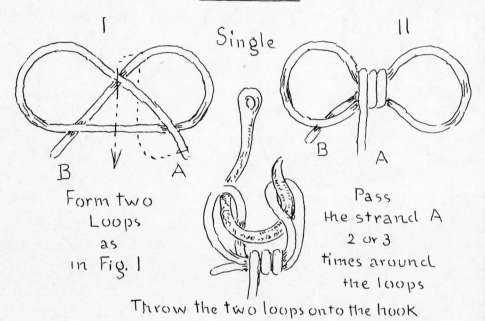

II

Pass
the strand A
2 or 3
times around
the loops

Throw the two loops onto the hook

Double

The two
Fore fingers form
the two loops
C & D

The line
is twisted by turning
the fingers two or three
times

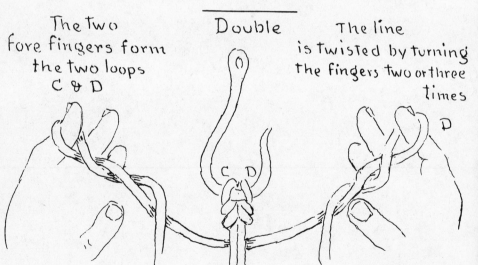

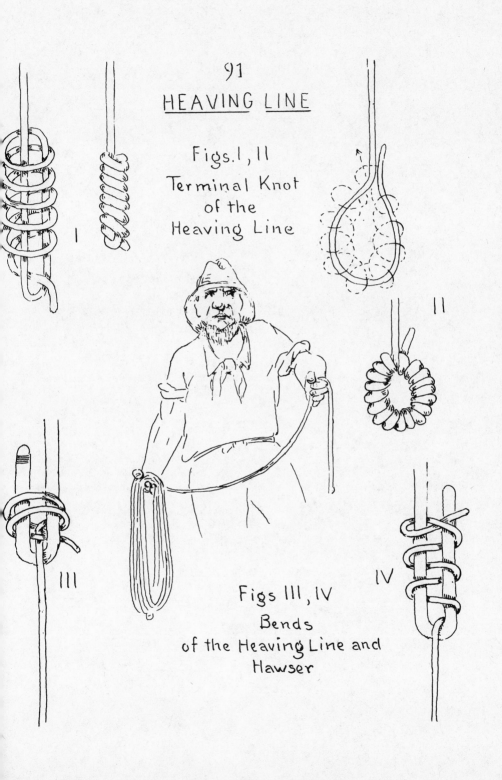

91

HEAVING LINE

Figs. I, II
Terminal Knot
of the
Heaving Line

I

II

III

IV

Figs III, IV
Bends
of the Heaving Line and
Hawser

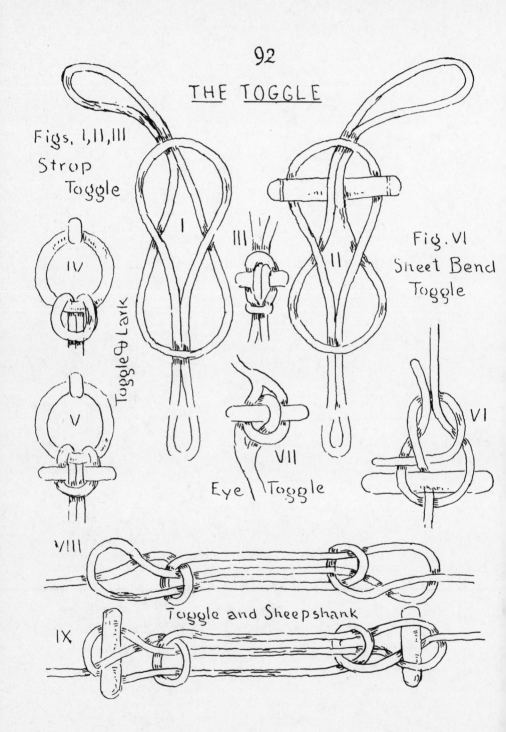

92

THE TOGGLE

Figs. I, II, III
Strop
Toggle

I

III

II

Fig. VI
Sheet Bend
Toggle

Toggle & Lark

IV

V

VII

Eye Toggle

VI

VIII

Toggle and Sheepshank

IX

MOORING

Over a Post

Tie an Overhand Knot on
the post
with the bight of the
line
and throw the
loop A over the post

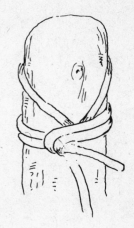

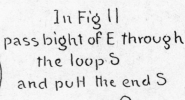

Through a Ring

In Fig I
pass the bight of S through
the loop E and pull
the end E

In Fig II
pass bight of E through
the loop S
and pull the end S

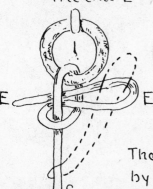

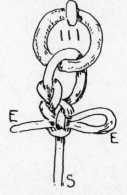

The knot is released
by pulling the end E
of III

MOORING

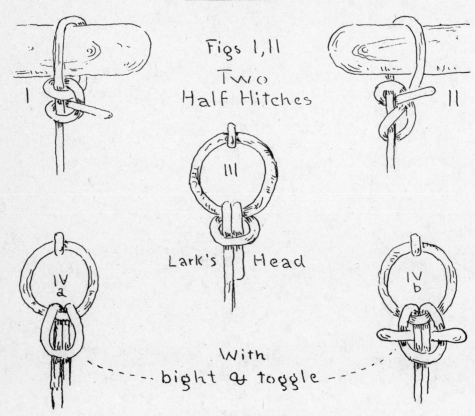

Figs I, II
Two
Half Hitches

Lark's Head

With
--- bight & toggle ---

Magnus Hitch

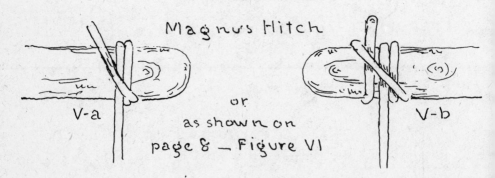

or
as shown on
page 8 — Figure VI

V-a   V-b

WHIPPING

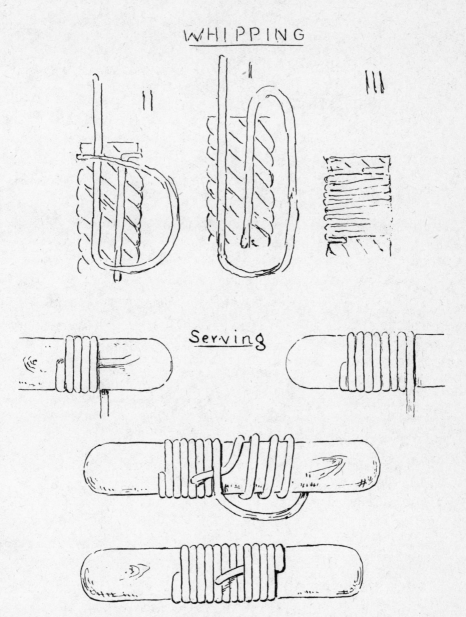

Serving

SPLICING

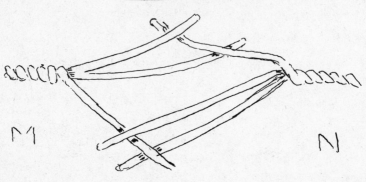

M   N

Unlay 7 or 8 strands of the two ropes M and N to be spliced   Arrange them in such manner that each strand of M lies between two strands of N and each of N lies between two strands of M.

Push the six strands close together and bind them temporarily with twine

SHORT SPLICE   Braiding

Each strand passes over the next one and then under the second beyond.

SHORT SPLICE

Twisting
the Strands

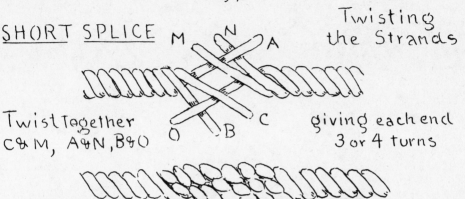

Twist Together
C & M, A & N, B & O

giving each end
3 or 4 turns

LONG SPLICE

Marry the strands as shown above

Unlay C to X
and replace it with M
& similarly
unlay O to Y
and replace It with B

Tie M & C together with an Overhand Knot
similarly tie together A & N and B & O
Taper the ends
and weave them into the strands of the rope

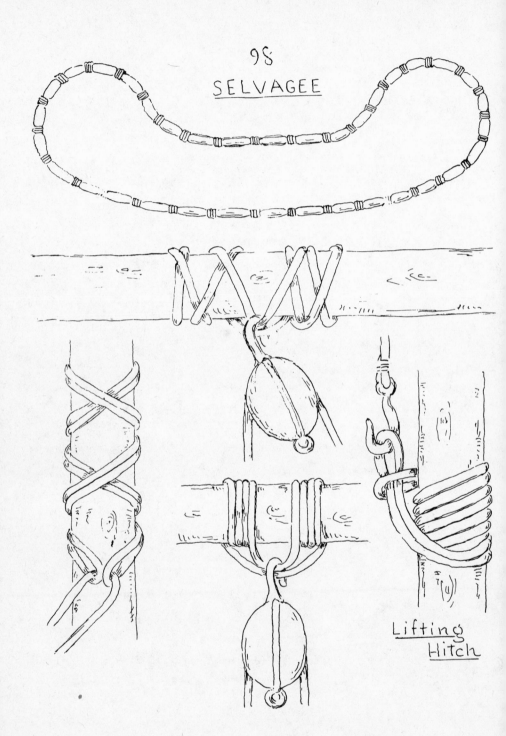

SELVAGEE

Lifting
Hitch

GROMMET

Carefully unlay a single strand of rope twelve times the diameter of the Grommet

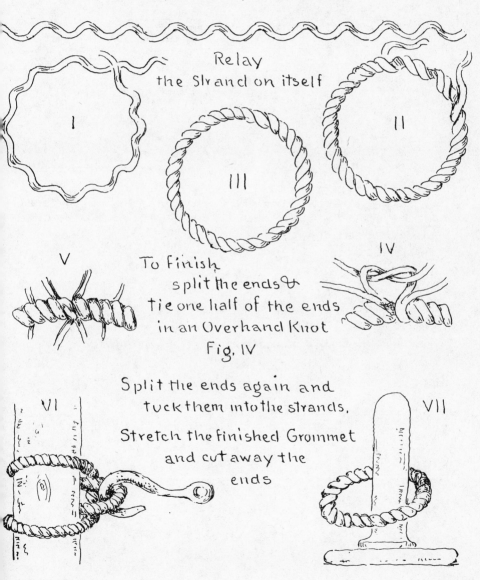

Relay
the Strand on itself

I

III

II

V

To finish
split the ends &
tie one half of the ends
in an Overhand Knot
Fig. IV

IV

Split the ends again and
tuck them into the strands.

Stretch the finished Grommet
and cut away the
ends

VI

VII

700

SHEEP SHANK

With both of the ends fast

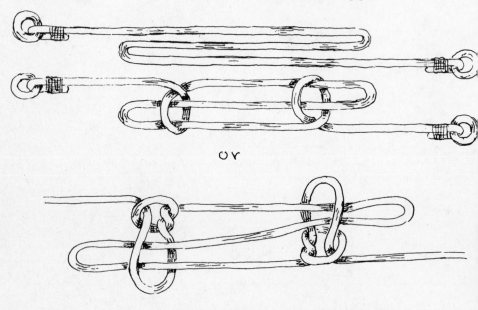

or

With the ends free

Overhand
Knot

Fig. of 8

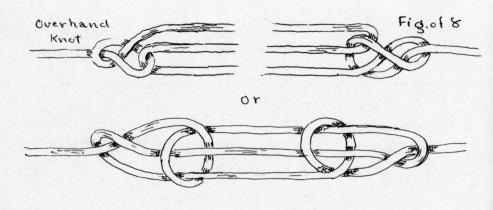

or

KNOTS
OF THE RANCH AND FARM

LASSO

THE HONDA or Hondo
An Eyelet tied with two Overhand Knots

Lasso

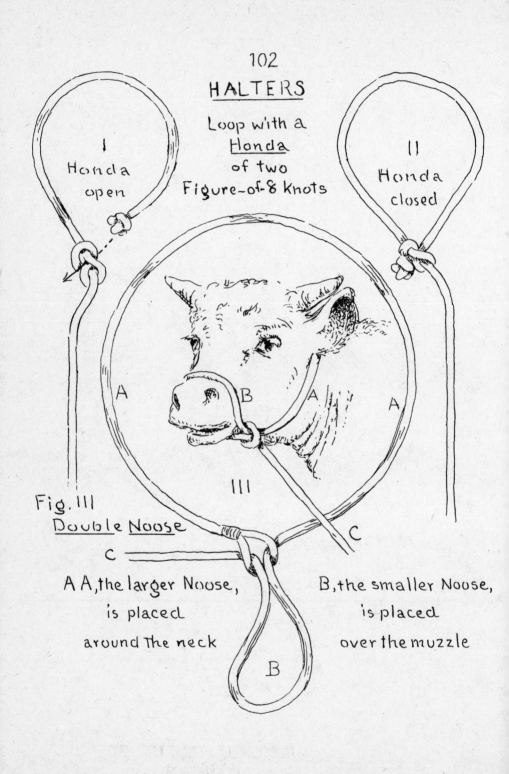

HALTERS

Loop with a
__Honda__
of two
__Figure-of-8 knots__

I
Honda
open

II
Honda
closed

A

B

A

A

III

Fig. III
__Double Noose__

C

C

A A, the larger Noose,
is placed
around the neck

B, the smaller Noose,
is placed
over the muzzle

B

HALTER and MANGER
KNOTS.

Figure-of-Eight
Noose

See page 41

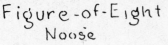
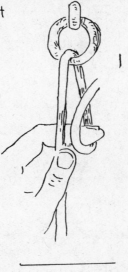
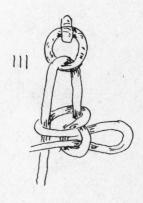

HACKAMORE TIE

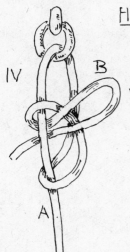

This is the
Buntline Hitch
which, by manipulation
of the parts A & B,
may be tied
as a Noose, Fig. IV
or
as a Loop, Fig. V

see page
34

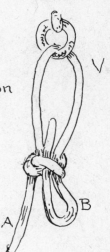

104

HALTER

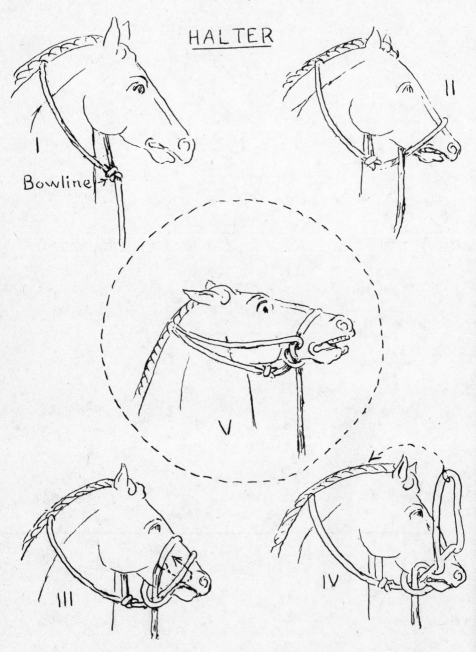

I

Bowline →

II

V

III

IV

SACK KNOTS

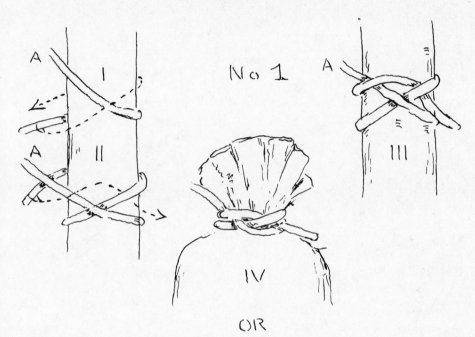

No 1

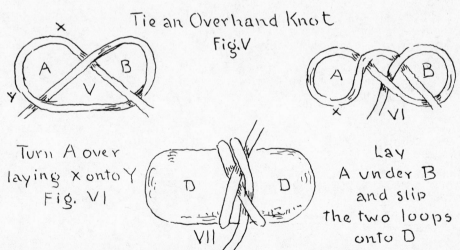

Tie an Overhand Knot
Fig.V

Turn A over
laying x onto Y
Fig. VI

Lay
A under B
and slip
the two loops
onto D

SACK KNOTS

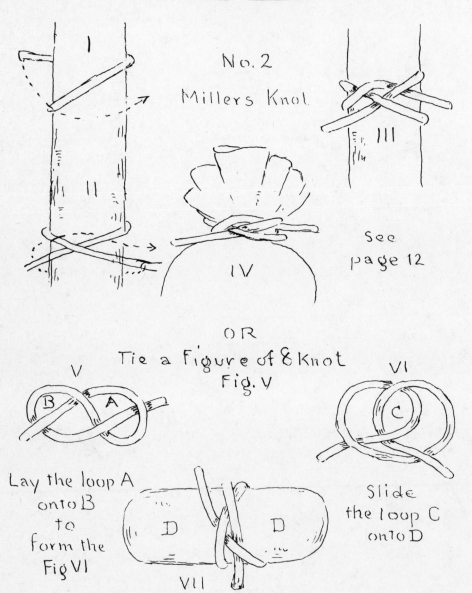

No. 2

Millers Knot

I

II

III

IV

See
page 12

OR

Tie a Figure of 8 Knot
Fig. V

V

B   A

VI

C

Lay the loop A
onto B
to
form the
Fig VI

VII

D   D

Slide
the loop C
onto D

SACK KNOTS

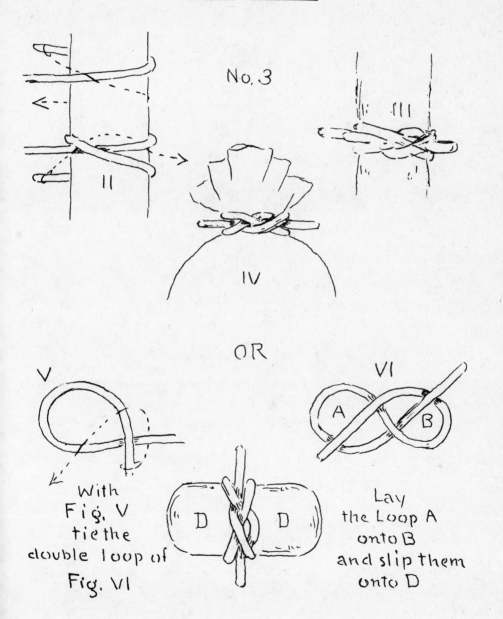

No. 3

II

III

IV

OR

V

VI

With
Fig. V
tie the
double loop of
Fig. VI

Lay
the Loop A
onto B
and slip them
onto D

SACK KNOTS

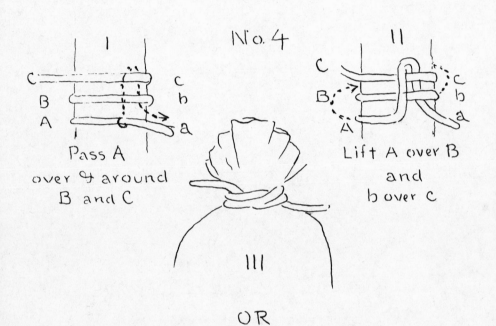

No. 4

I

Pass A over & around B and C

II

Lift A over B and b over c

III

OR

Tie a Blood Knot Fig. IV

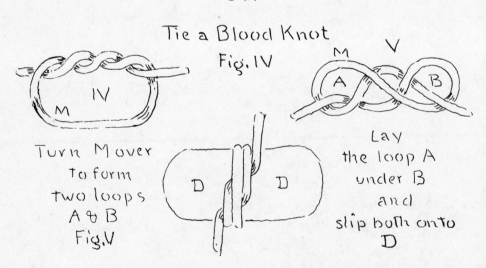

IV

Turn M over to form two loops A & B Fig. V

V

Lay the loop A under B and slip both onto D

109

DIAMOND HITCH

A compensating device for
    securing the pack
      on a horse

The rope is adjusted to form
    a quadrangle
    on the top of the pack.

The strain that tends to pull A & B apart
    is held in check
    by a counter-strain at
      the points
        C & D

JAR SLING

I

II

III

A

B

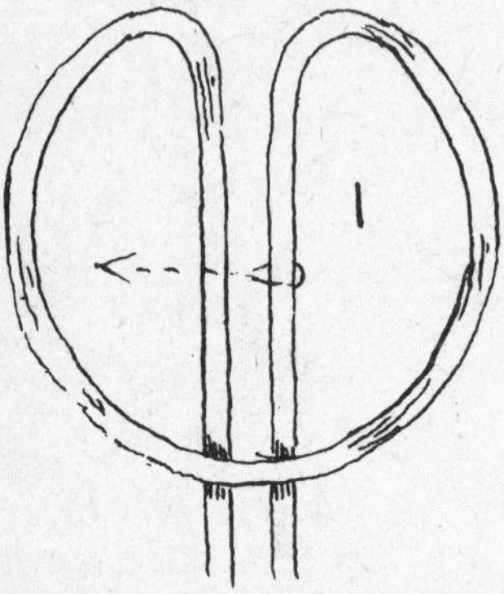

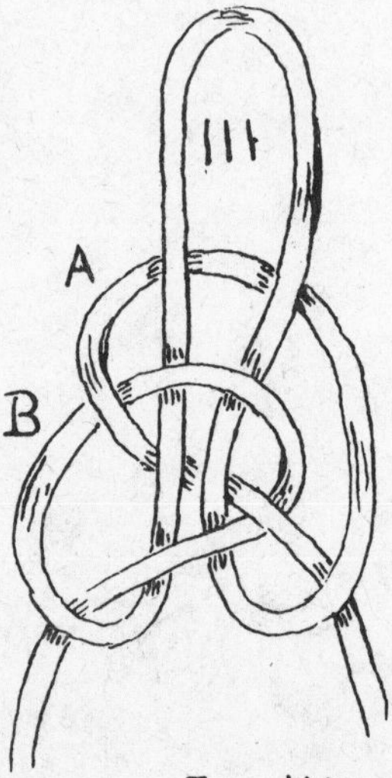

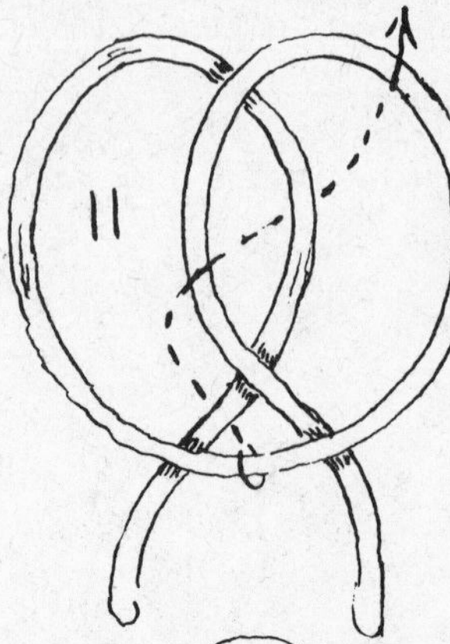

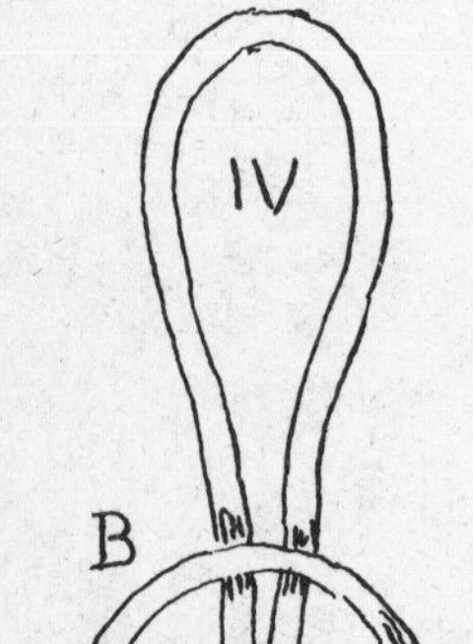

In Fig. III
pass the loop A down
to the position
shown in
Fig. IV

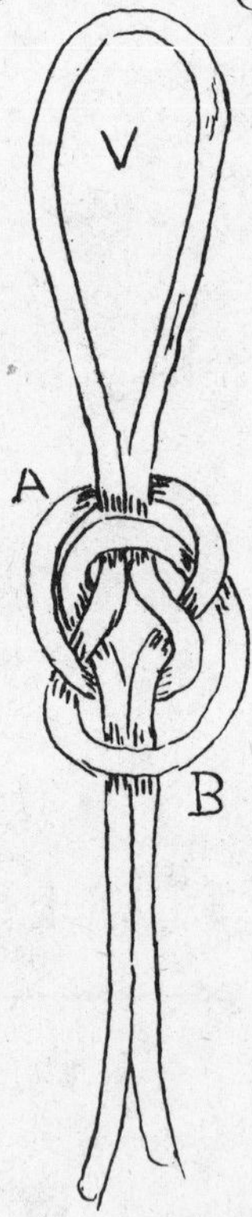

IV

B

A

In Fig IV
pass the loop B
down to
the position of B
in
Fig. V

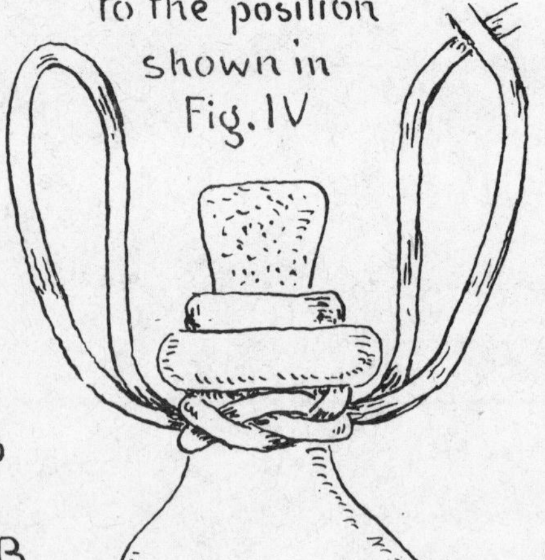

V

A

B

SLINGS

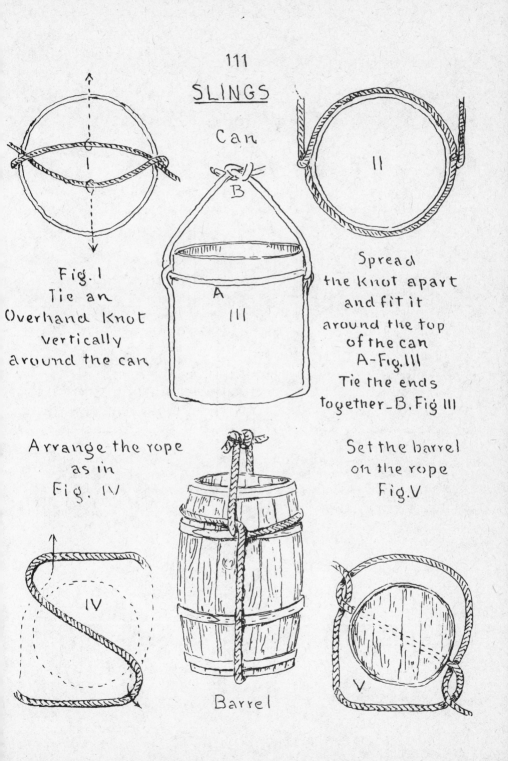

Can

Fig. I
Tie an
Overhand Knot
vertically
around the can

Spread
the Knot apart
and fit it
around the top
of the can
A-Fig. III
Tie the ends
together—B. Fig III

Arrange the rope
as in
Fig. IV

Set the barrel
on the rope
Fig. V

Barrel

112

LADDERS

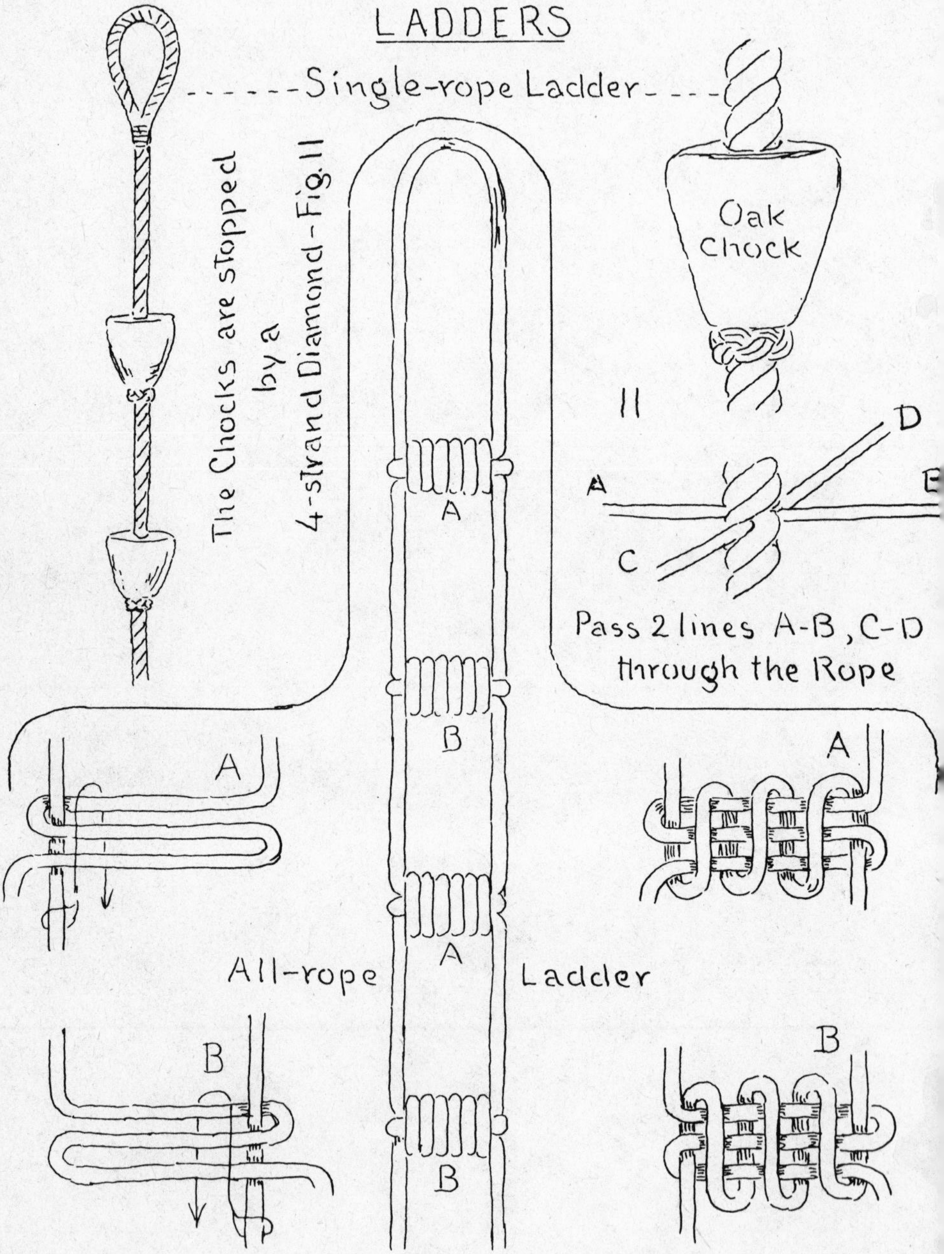

The Chocks are stopped by a 4-strand Diamond – Fig. 11

Oak Chock

11

Pass 2 lines A-B, C-D through the Rope

A

B

A

All-rope Ladder

B

A

B

A

B

113
ANGLER'S KNOTS
Line and Leader

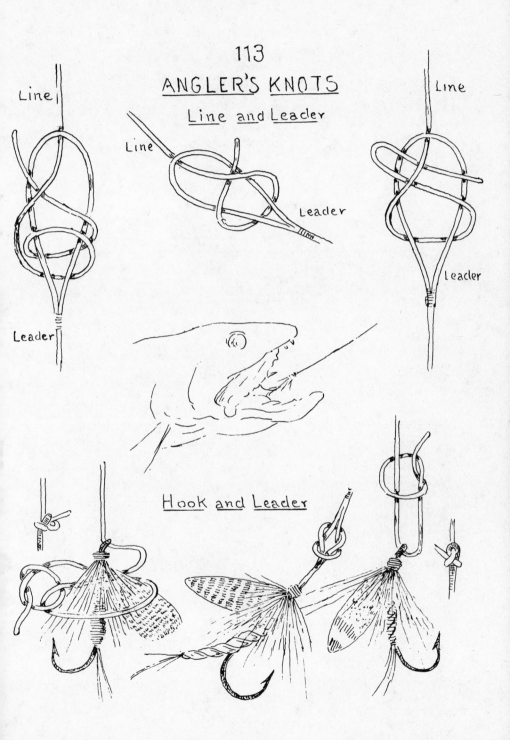

Line

Line

Leader

Line

Line

Leader

Leader

Leader

Hook and Leader

TYING LEADERS

Barrel Knot

I

Water Knot

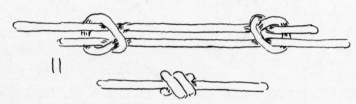

II

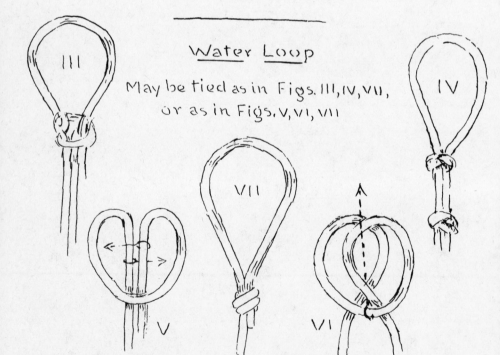

Water Loop

May be tied as in Figs. III, IV, VII,
or as in Figs. V, VI, VII

III

IV

VII

V

VI

For Angler's Loop see page 43

TYING FLIES

A simple and effective
artificial fly
may be tied with a fish hook,
a length of colored silk,
and a hackle from the neck of a cock.

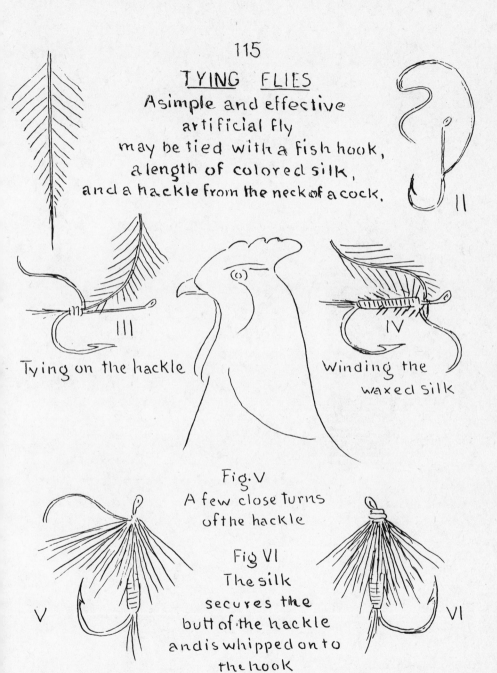

II

III
Tying on the hackle

IV
Winding the
waxed silk

Fig. V
A few close turns
of the hackle

Fig VI
The silk
secures the
butt of the hackle
and is whipped on to
the hook

V   VI

to form the head of the fly _ A drop of varnish on the head

FISHERMAN'S NET

The Knot
is the same as
the Sheet Bend, Bowline &c.
It is a Half Hitch
combined
with
a Loop

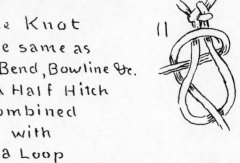

Fig.I - the Loop
Fig.II Loop and
Half Hitch

Fig III A B C
represents the
Loop

Fig IV
The end D
ties
the Half Hitch

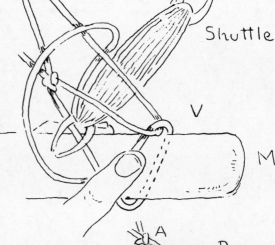

Shuttle

Mesh

V

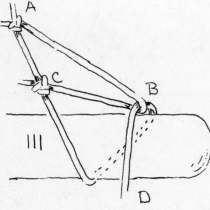

III

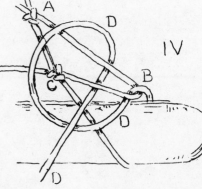

IV

117
CIRCULAR NET

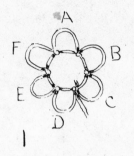

Fig. I
Tie 6 loops
on a centre loop

Fig II
Tie 2 knots on each loop

I

II

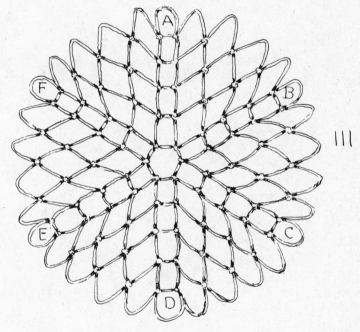

III

Fig III
The diameter of the net
increases
by tying 2 knots
on each of the loops that lie on
the three lines
AD-BE-CF

This net can he
tied

TENNIS NET

without mesh or
shuttle

Tied with short lines — A, A

A   A   A   A

The net should be hung on a wire rope
which is fixed permanently in position

The net and its fringe should be 2 ft. 6 in. deep
and, when hung, 6 in. above the ground

NETTING

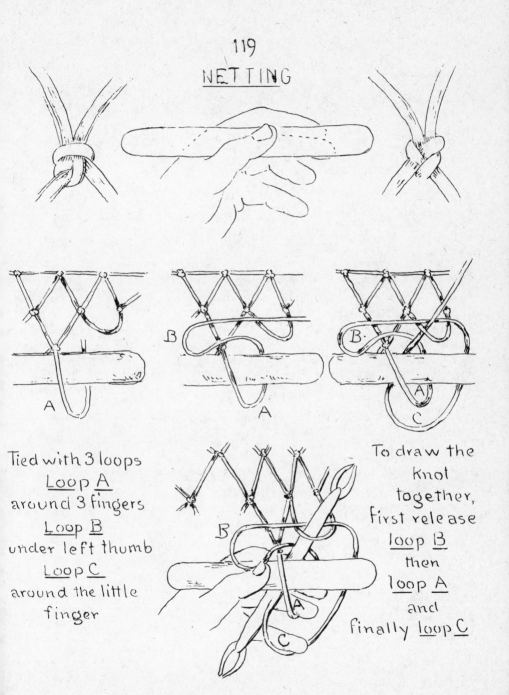

Tied with 3 loops
Loop **A**
around 3 fingers
Loop **B**
under left thumb
Loop **C**
around the little
finger

To draw the
knot
together,
first release
loop **B**
then
loop **A**
and
finally loop **C**

TYING PACKAGES

Front

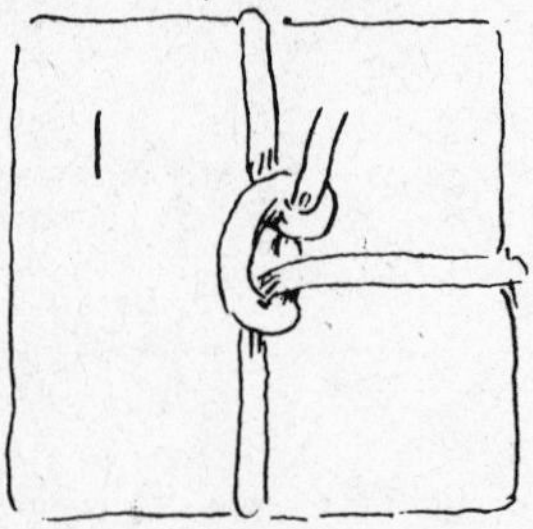

Back

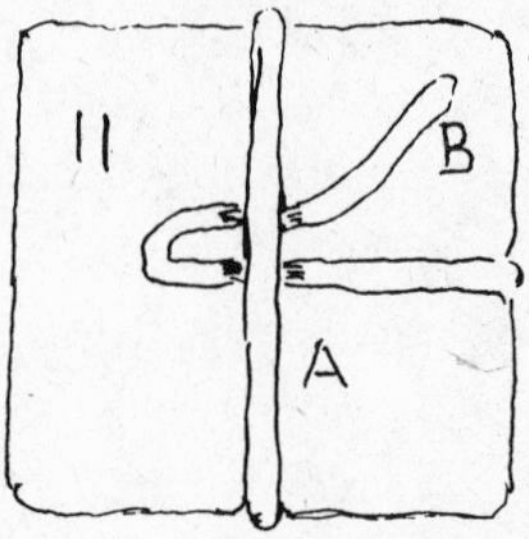

Fig. I
Begin with the Packers' Noose

Fig II
Pass the bight of the line under the strand A

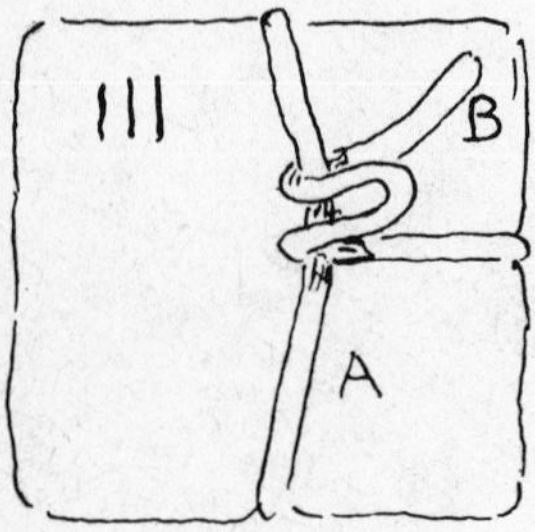

Back

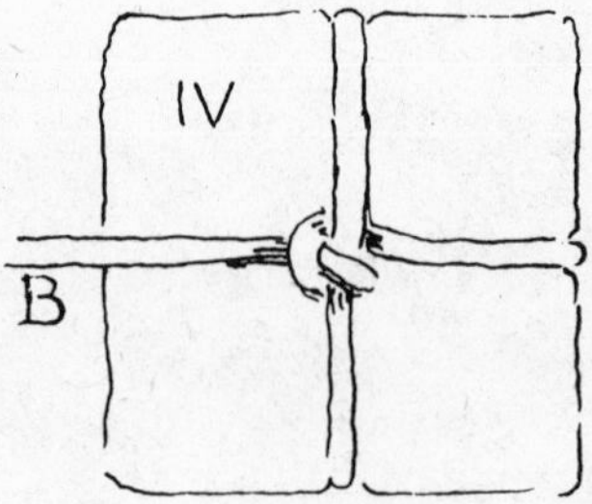

Back

Fig. III
With the bight draw the strand A taut

Fig. IV
Pass the end B through the bight and draw the knot taut

Figs. V and VI
Finish with two or three Half Hitches

Front

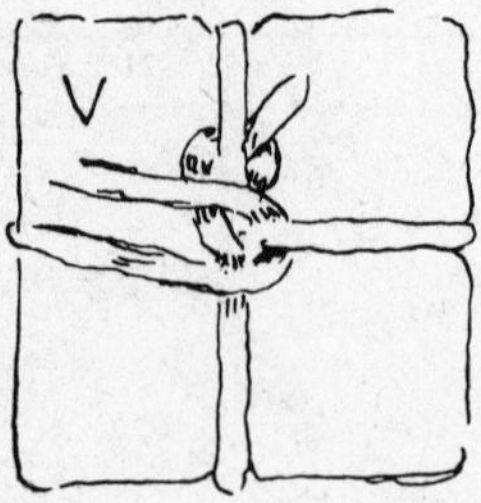

Front

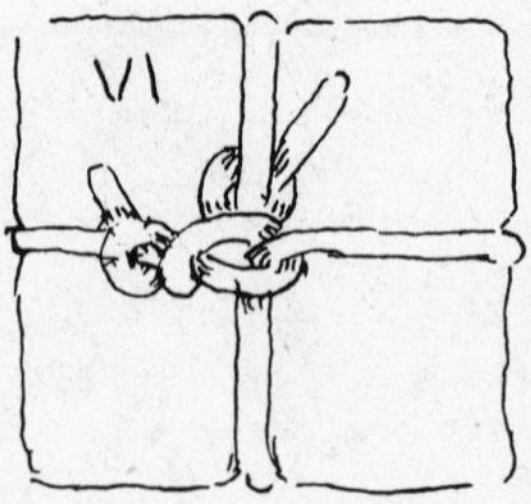

TYING
PACKAGES

Fig 1
Introduced here as a not-too-difficult puzzle
{ To tie a 4-strand package
with a single line, the beginning and the end not shown }

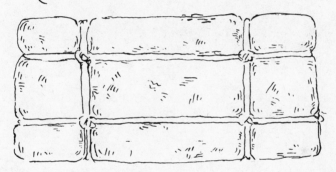

Diamond Tie

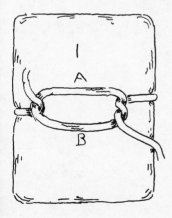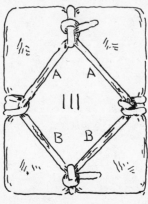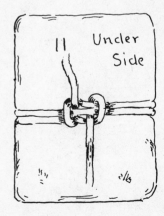

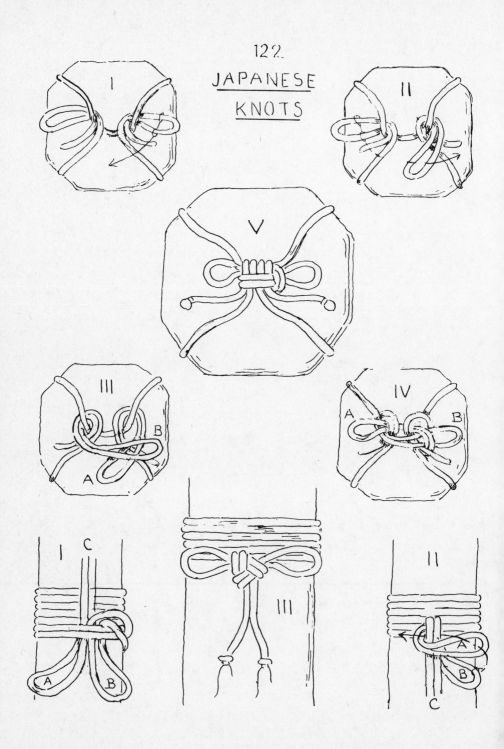

122.

JAPANESE
KNOTS

123
KNIFE — LANYARD

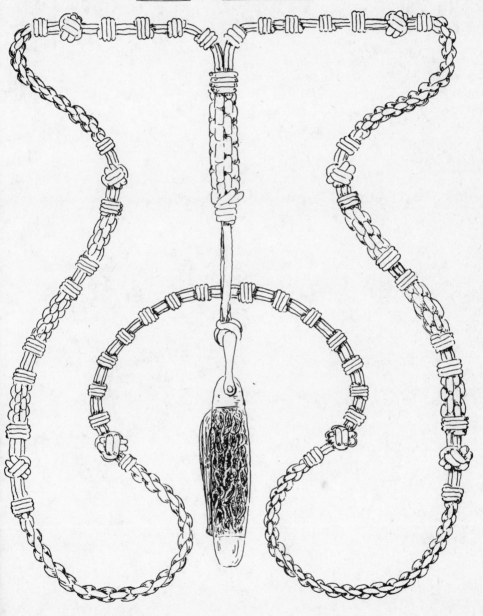

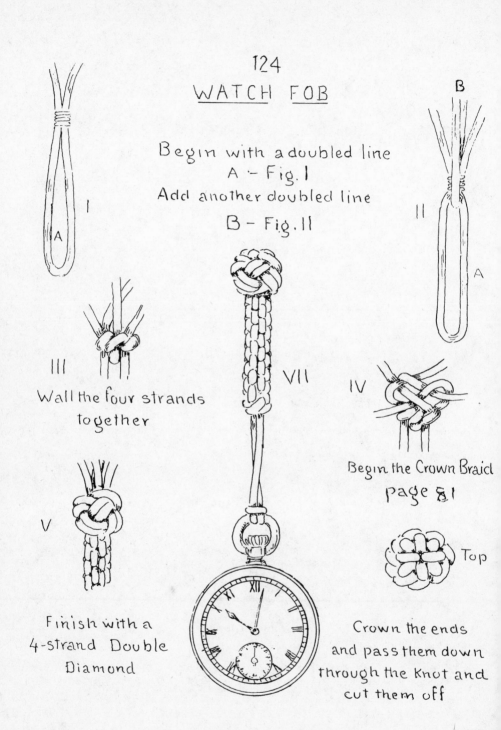

124

WATCH FOB

Begin with a doubled line
A - Fig. I
Add another doubled line
B - Fig. II

I

A

B

II

A

III

Wall the four strands
together

IV

Begin the Crown Braid
page 81

VII

V

Finish with a
4-strand Double
Diamond

Top

Crown the ends
and pass them down
through the knot and
cut them off

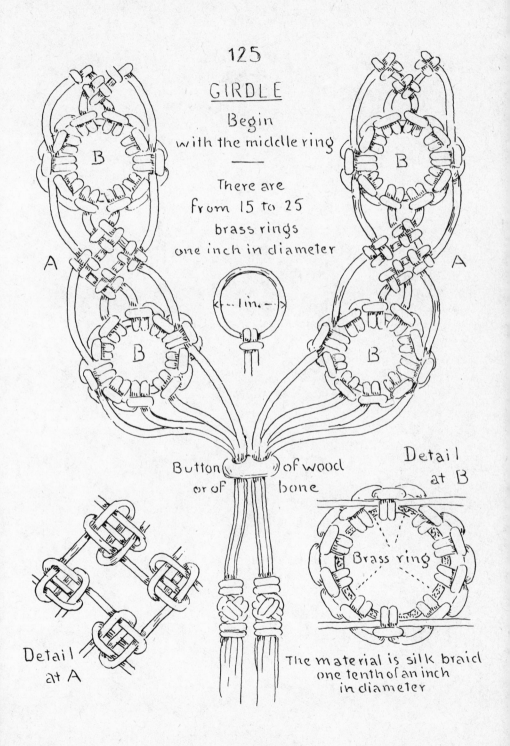

125

GIRDLE

Begin
with the middle ring
—
There are
from 15 to 25
brass rings
one inch in diameter

|<-- 1 in. -->|

A

B

B

B

B

A

Button of wood
or of bone

Detail at B

Brass ring

Detail
at A

The material is silk braid
one tenth of an inch
in diameter

LEATHER FASTENING
FOR
A Girdle

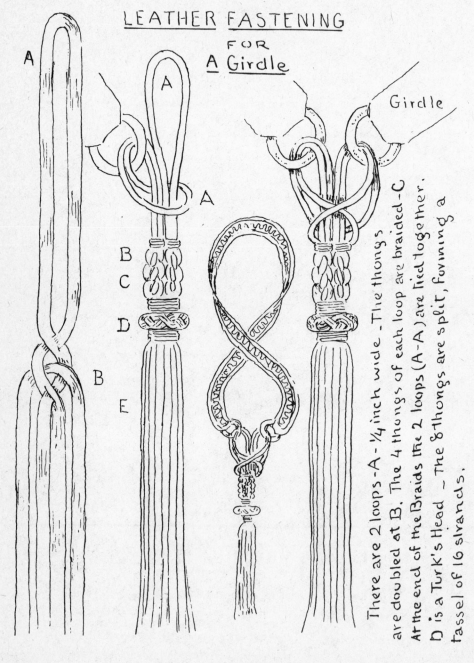

A

A

A

Girdle

B

C

D

B

E

There are 2 loops - A - ¼ inch wide - The thongs
are doubled at B. The 4 thongs of each loop are braided - C
At the end of the Braids the 2 loops (A-A) are tied together.
D is a Turk's Head - The 8 thongs are split, forming a
tassel of 16 strands.

LEATHER BELT
and
BUCKLE

Fig. 1
A - Part of Belt
slit into
three Strands — See page 86

Fig. 1
B - Two iron or
brass rings

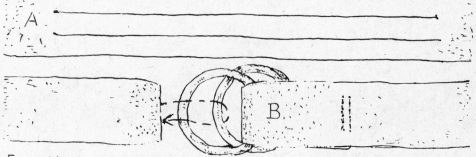

A

B

Fig II - A - The strands braided - B - The buckle fastened

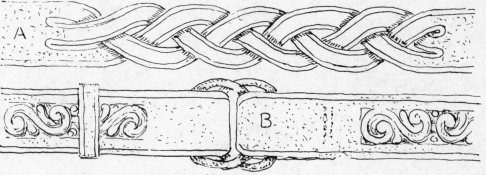

A

B

Fig. III - The inside of Buckle — The rings enlarged
to show method more
clearly

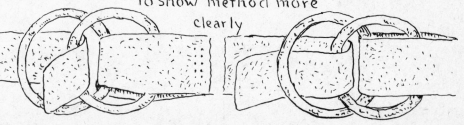

MACRAME KNOTS

These are
The Square Knot, the Half Hitch and the Granny
tied around
one or more idle lines
drawn taut

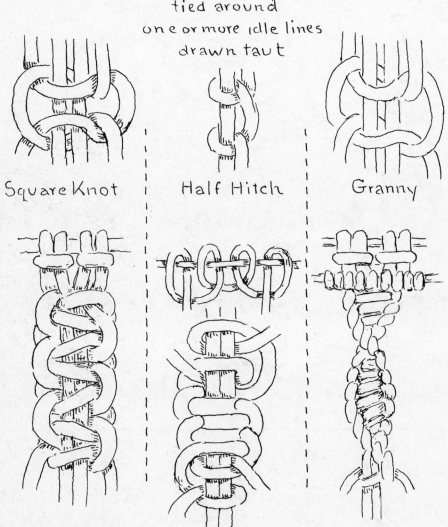

Square Knot   Half Hitch   Granny

129

MACRAME KNOTS

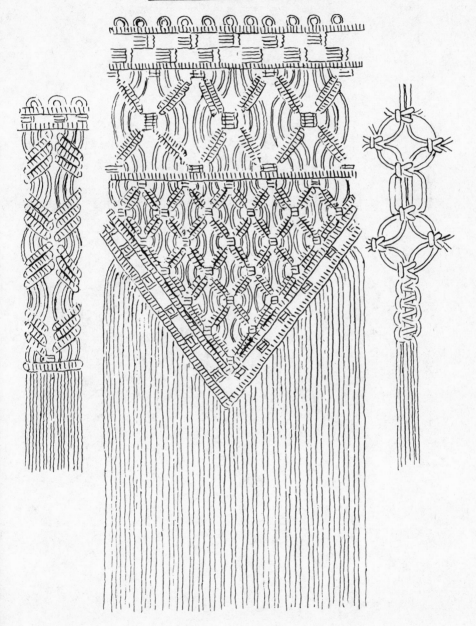

TATTING LOOP

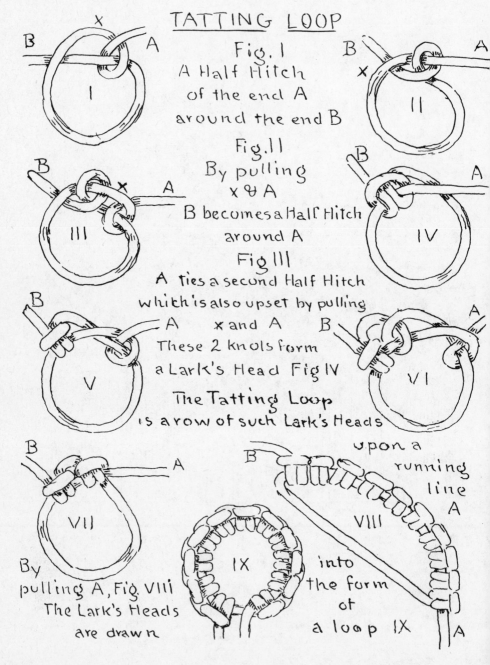

Fig. I
A Half Hitch
of the end A
around the end B

Fig. II
By pulling
x & A
B becomes a Half Hitch
around A

Fig III
A ties a second Half Hitch
which is also upset by pulling
x and A
These 2 knots form
a Lark's Head Fig IV

The Tatting Loop
is a row of such Lark's Heads
upon a
running
line

By
pulling A, Fig. VIII
The Lark's Heads
are drawn
into
the form
of
a loop IX

TATTING

Insertion

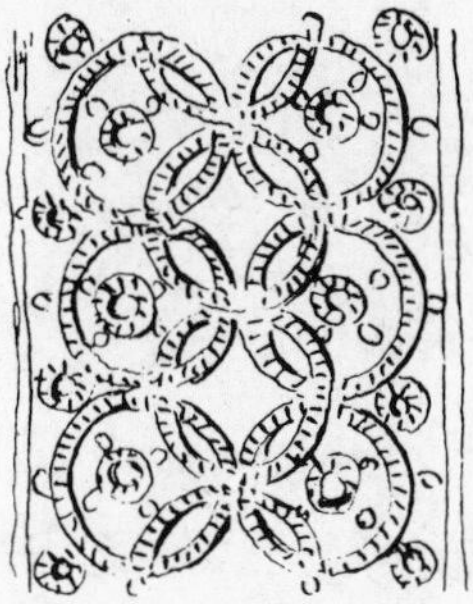

Fig I Loop

Insertion

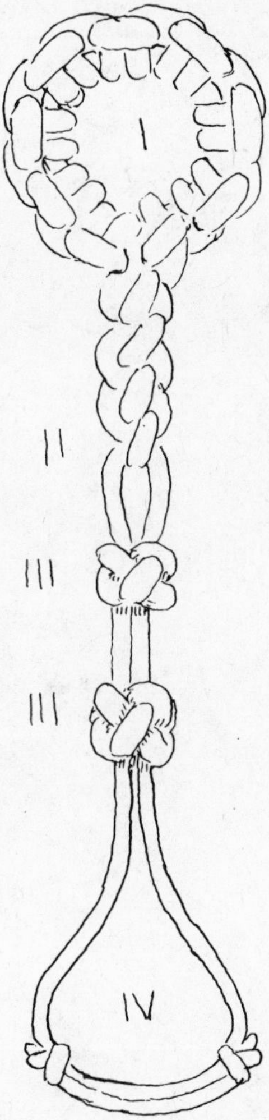

Fig. II
Round Braid

See page 77

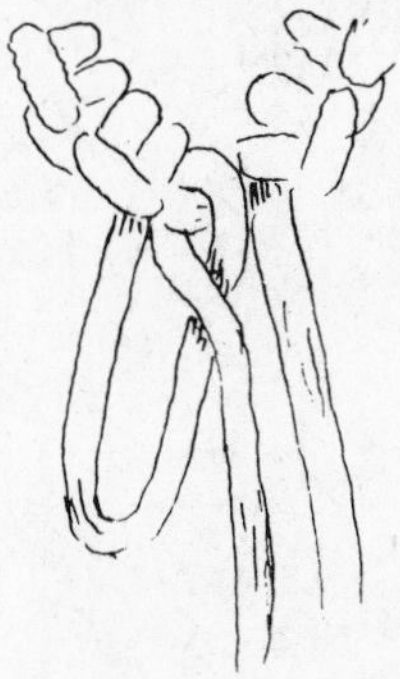

Fig III
Diamond Knot

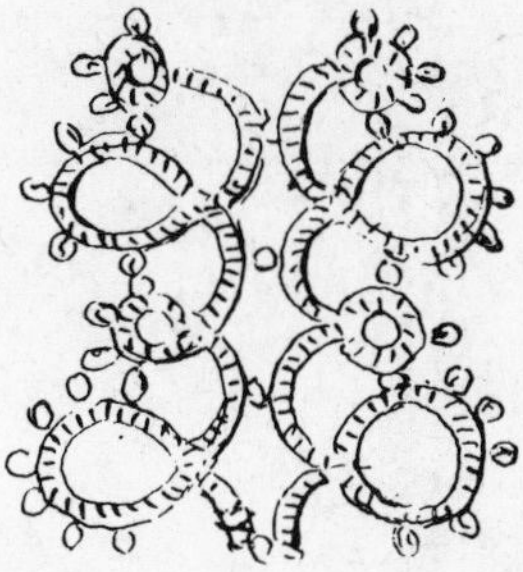

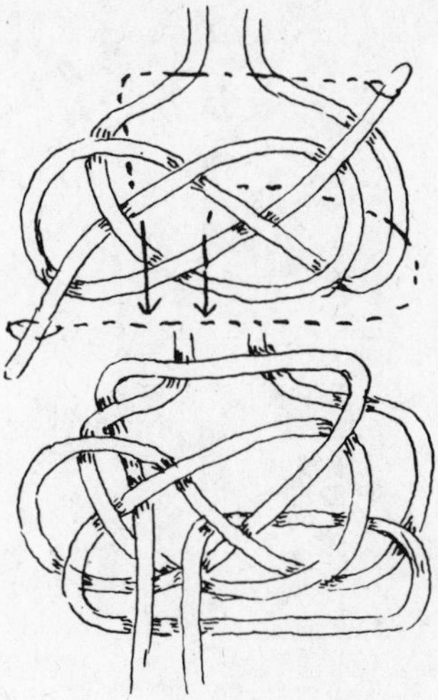

I

II

III

III

IV

Lace

Fig. IV
Water Knot

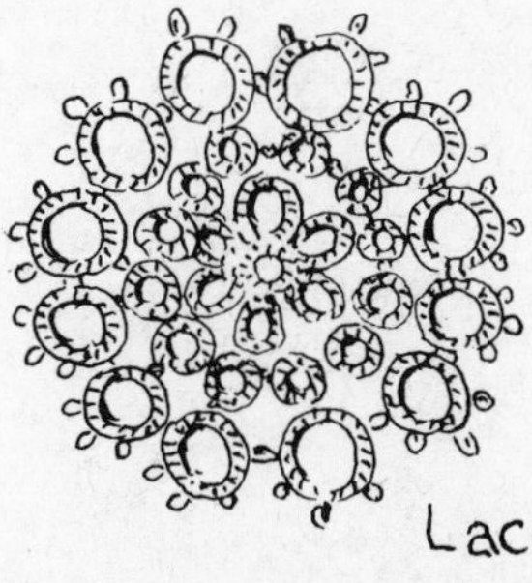

Lace

BOOK COVER

BOOK COVER

Turkish Knot

Persian Knot

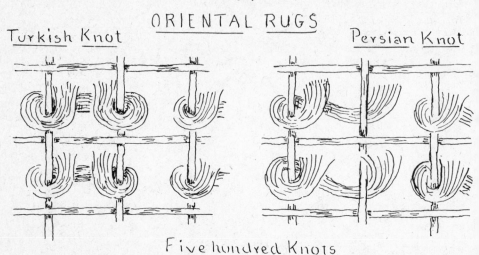

Five hundred knots
to the square inch are not unusual

KNOTS
IN
HERALDRY

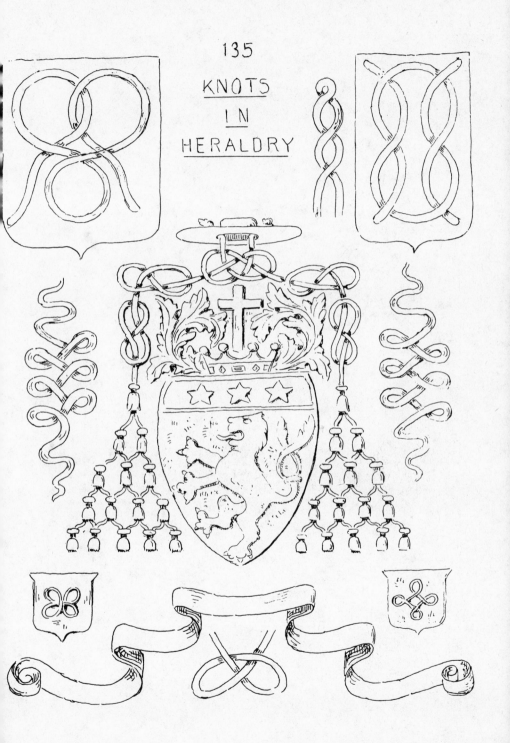

CHINESE KNOT

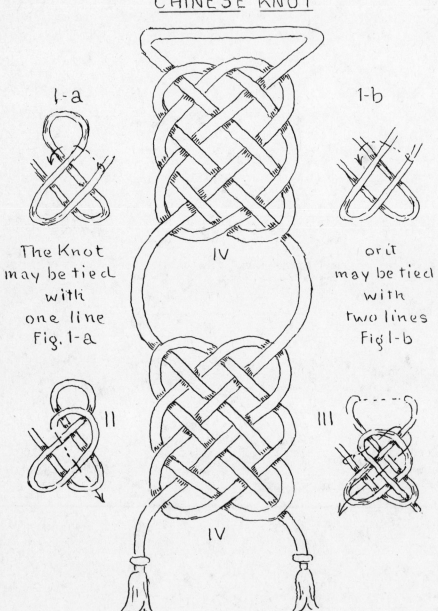

1-a

1-b

The Knot
may be tied
with
one line
Fig. 1-a

or it
may be tied
with
two lines
Fig 1-b

IV

II

III

IV

ADDING STRANDS to the CHINESE KNOT

I

II

V

III

IV

DEVELOPMENT
of Interlacings of any number of strands

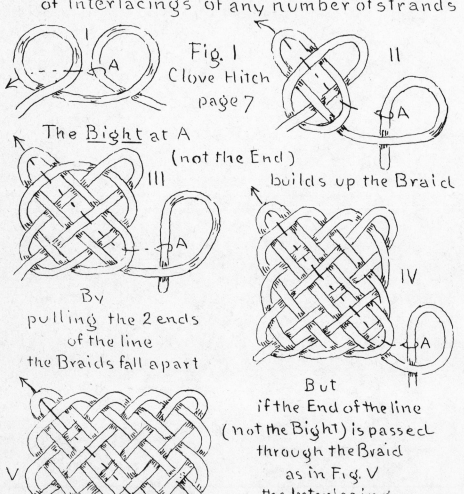

Fig. I
Clove Hitch
page 7

I

A

II

A

The <u>Bight</u> at A
(not the End)
builds up the Braid

III

A

IV

A

By
pulling the 2 ends
of the line
the Braids fall apart

V

But
if the End of the line
(not the Bight) is passed
through the Braid
as in Fig. V
the Interlacing
cannot fall apart
and the work can be so ended
at any one of its stages.

140

TEMPLE ORNAMENTS

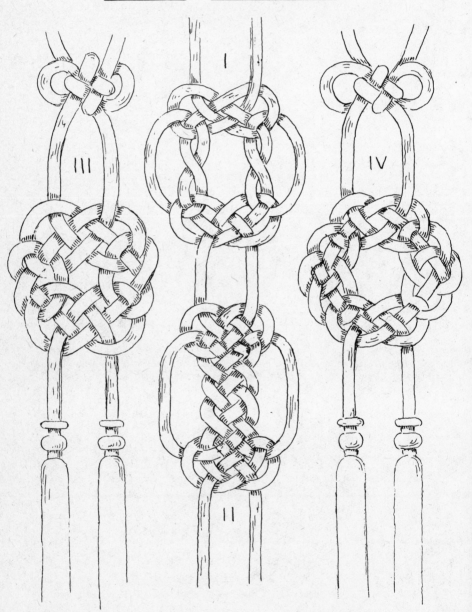

141

Details of Temple Ornaments

A - begins all four knots

B - belongs with Knots I & II

C - belongs with Knots III & IV

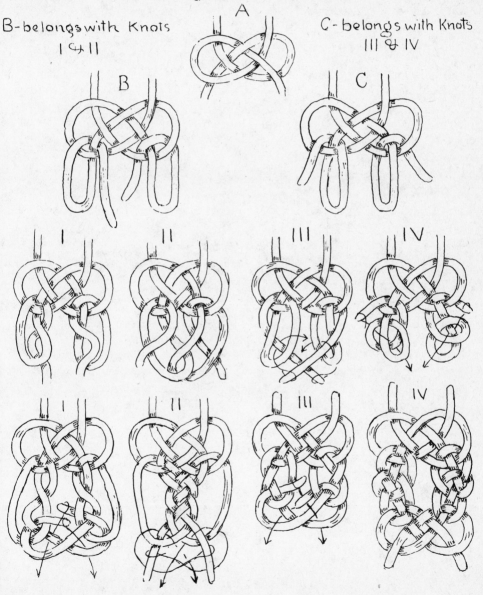

142

ORNAMENTAL FORMS
based on the
Overhand Knot

143

DOUBLE CARRICK

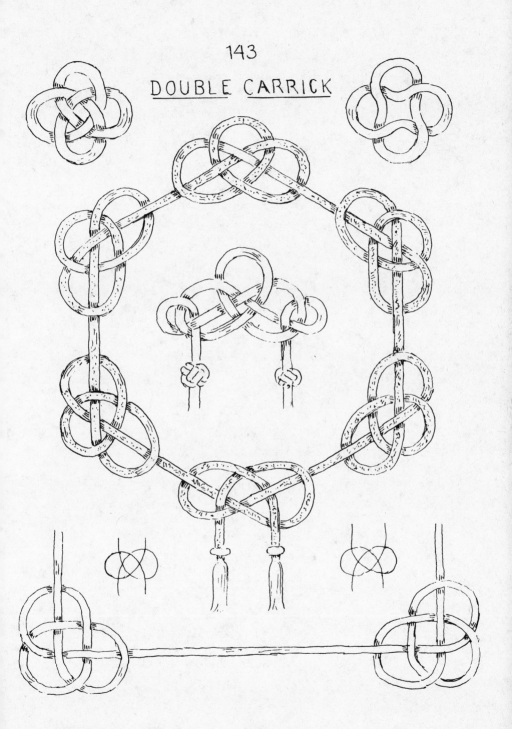

ORNAMENTAL KNOTS

CELTIC KNOTS

146

CELTIC
INTERLACINGS

Panels
II, III, IV & V
are modifications
of panel I

II

III

I

A

B

C

D

Fig. A
may be changed to B
or, to

Fig. C
can be changed to D

IV

V

CELTIC KNOTS

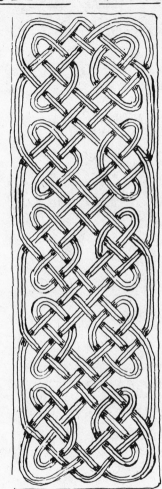

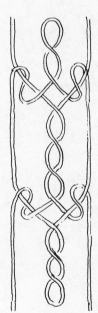

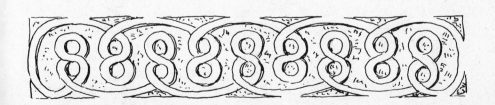

JAPANESE KNOTS

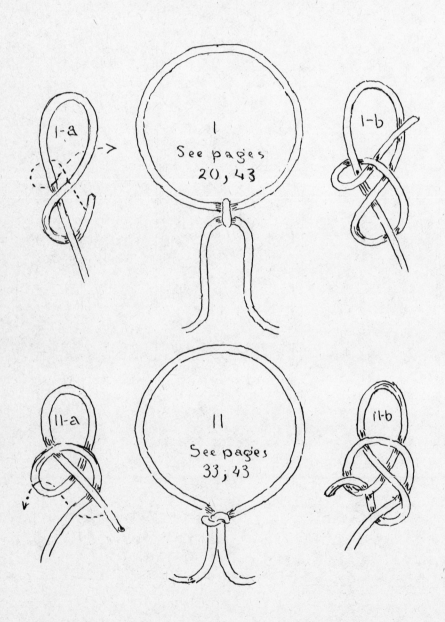

I-a

1
See pages
20, 43

I-b

II-a

II
See pages
33, 43

II-b

149
JAPANESE CROWN KNOT

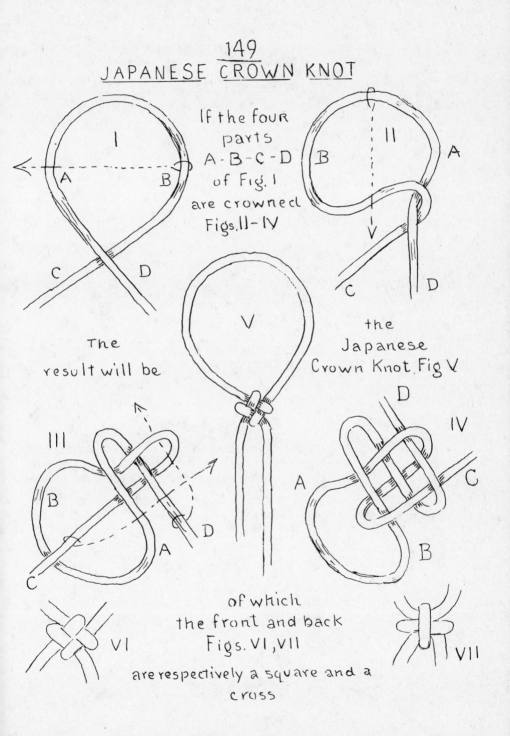

If the four
parts
A-B-C-D
of Fig. I
are crowned
Figs. II–IV

The
result will be

the
Japanese
Crown Knot. Fig V

of which
the front and back
Figs. VI, VII
are respectively a square and a
cross

150)

ANOTHER METHOD

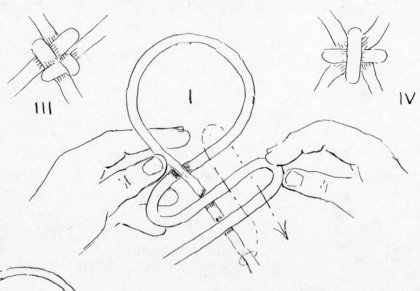

III   I   IV

II

In the museum in Salem, Mass,
where many Japanese knots are shown,
this knot is labelled
the

SUCCESS KNOT

The square Fig. III
and
the cross Fig. IV,
when combined, Fig. V,
form the word.
KANAU
"The wish realized"

V

ANOTHER METHOD

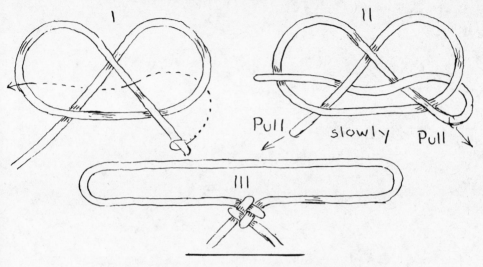

I II

Pull   slowly   Pull

III

DOUBLE SUCCESS KNOT

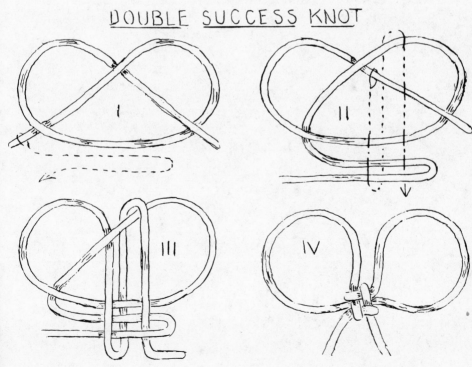

I II

III IV

152

JAPANESE KNOTS

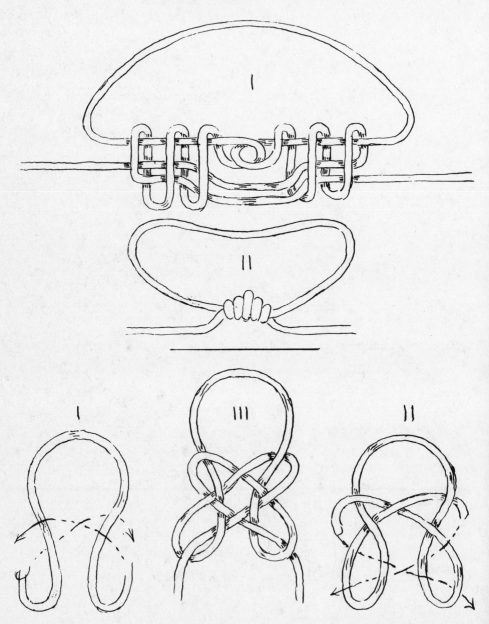

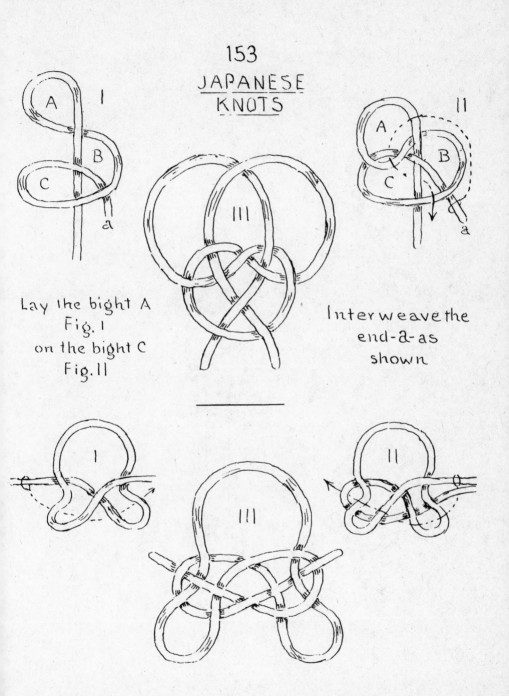

153
JAPANESE
KNOTS

I

A

B

C

a

Lay the bight A
Fig. I
on the bight C
Fig. II

III

II

A

B

C

a

Interweave the
end-a-as
shown

I

II

III

154

JAPANESE KNOTS

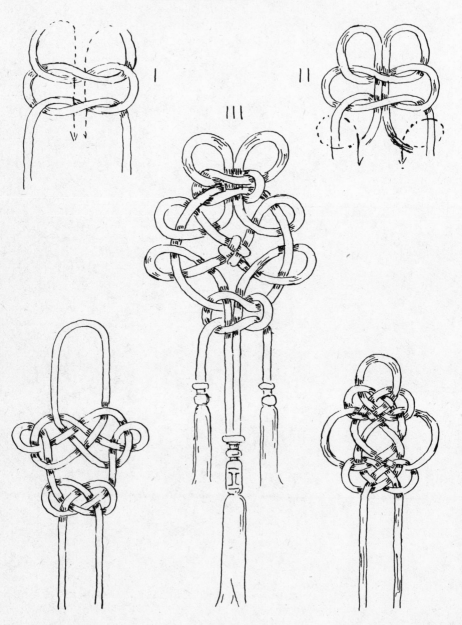

ORIENTAL KNOTS

Suggesting the outline of Flowers and of Insects &c

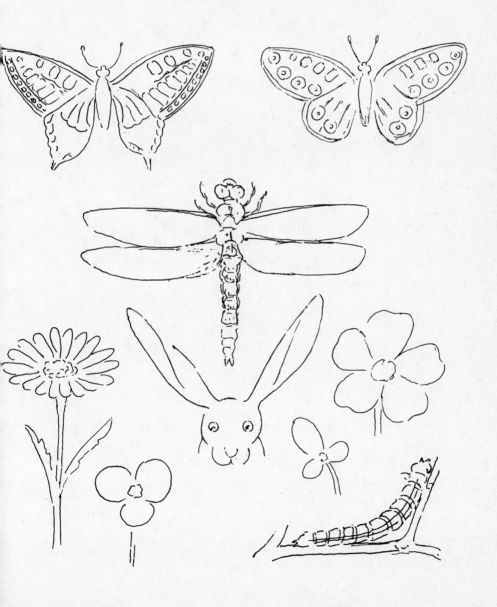

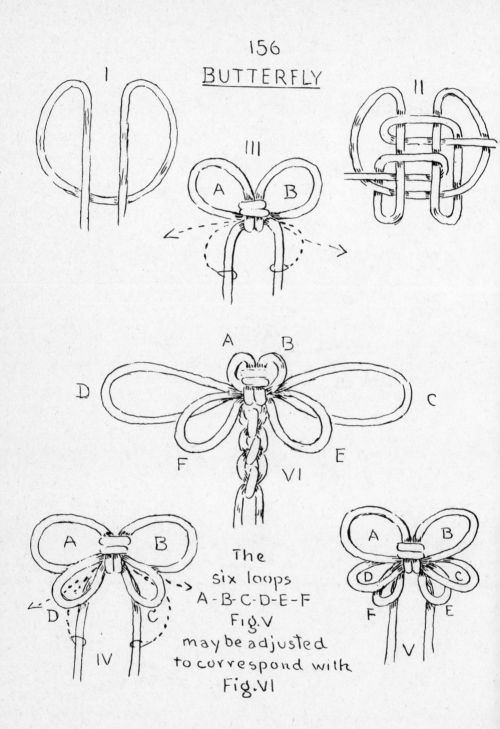

156
BUTTERFLY

I

III

A   B

II

A   B

D   C

F   E

VI

A   B

D   C

IV

The
six loops
A - B - C - D - E - F
Fig. V
may be adjusted
to correspond with
Fig. VI

A   B

D   C

F   E

V

BUTTERFLY

Fig I-a

The Double-triangular Knot, page 171.
Its parts may be adjusted
to form Fig I-b

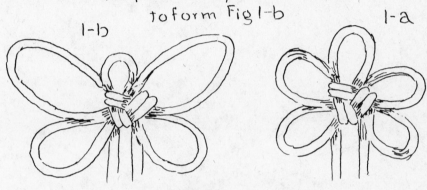

1-b   1-a

Fig. II-a

The Hexagonal Knot, page 176.
Its parts may also be adjusted
to form
a Butterfly Knot

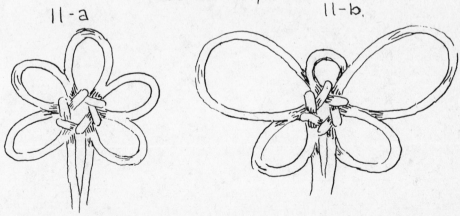

II-a   II-b.

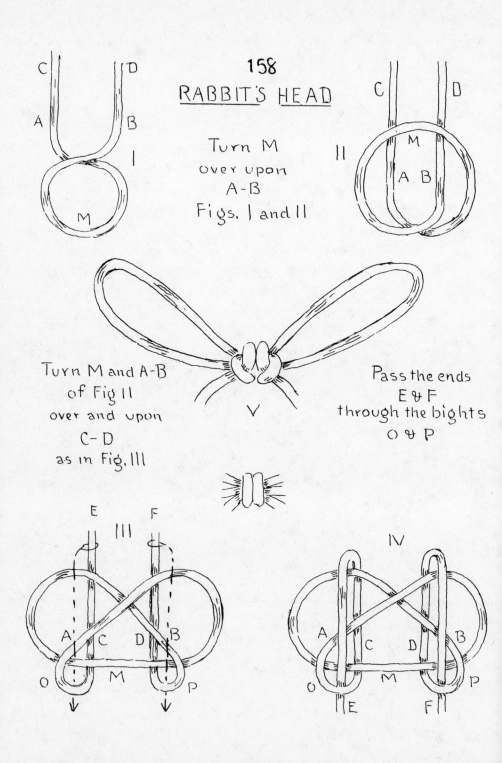

158
RABBIT'S HEAD

C D

A B

I

Turn M
over upon
A-B
Figs. I and II

II

C D

M

A B

Turn M and A-B
of Fig II
over and upon
C-D
as in Fig. III

V

Pass the ends
E & F
through the bights
O & P

E F

III

A C D B

O M P

IV

A C D B

O M P

E F

THE DRAGON FLY

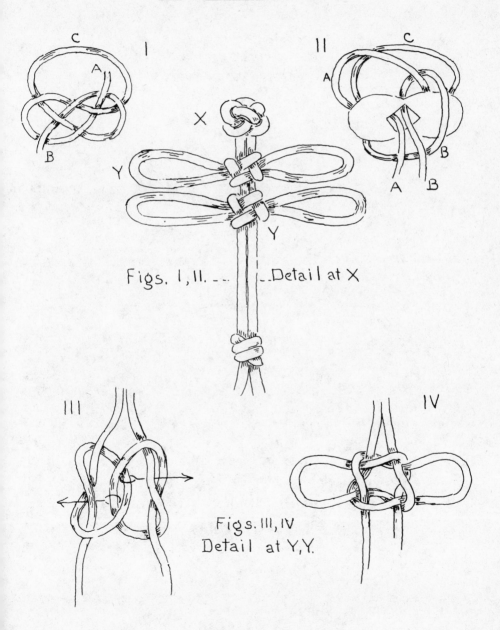

Figs. I, II. _____ Detail at X

Figs. III, IV
Detail at Y,Y.

INSECT

In the Museum in Salem Mass.
are two Japanese Knots with the label
"Insect"

I

One of them, Fig I, is a

three-strand Sennit, page 72
and probably represents an

EARTHWORM

III

The other, Fig. II,
is a combination of two
Macramé Square Knots,
see page 128,
and may possibly represent a

II

BEETLE

Fig. II suggests a method
for tying a

CATERPILLAR

IV

Fig. III is a series of Square
Knots & spaces
around two idle lines on which
the knots are free to run,
By sliding the
Knots together, Fig. IV is
the result

MODIFICATIONS
of the
Overhand Noose

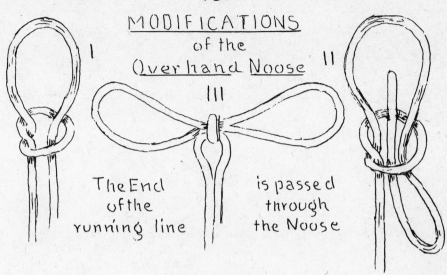

III

The End
of the
running line

is passed
through
the Noose

TREFOIL

The Bight of
the fixed line

is passed
through the Noose

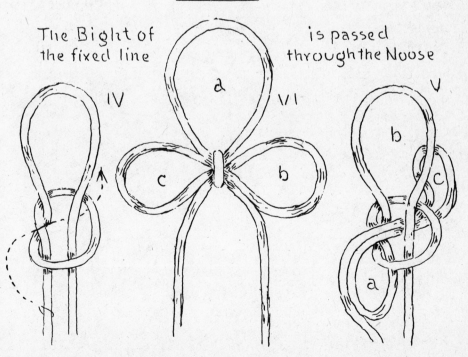

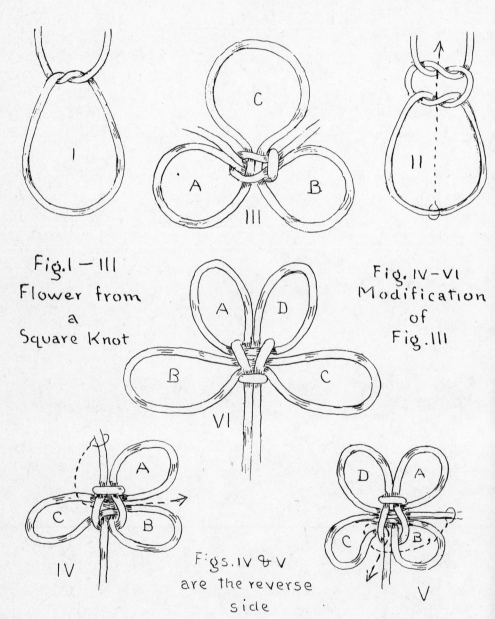

Fig. I — III
Flower from
a
Square Knot

Fig. IV-VI
Modification
of
Fig. III

Figs. IV & V
are the reverse
side

FLOWER KNOT

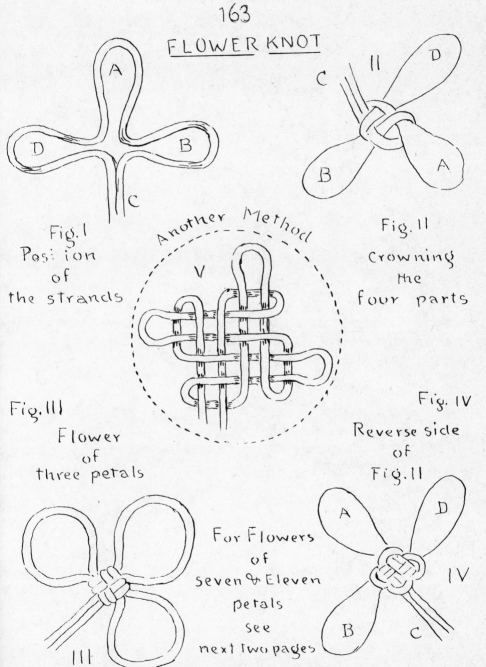

Fig. I
Position
of
the strands

Another Method

V

Fig. II
Crowning
the
four parts

Fig. III
Flower
of
three petals

Fig. IV
Reverse side
of
Fig. II

For Flowers
of
Seven & Eleven
petals
see
next two pages

III

IV

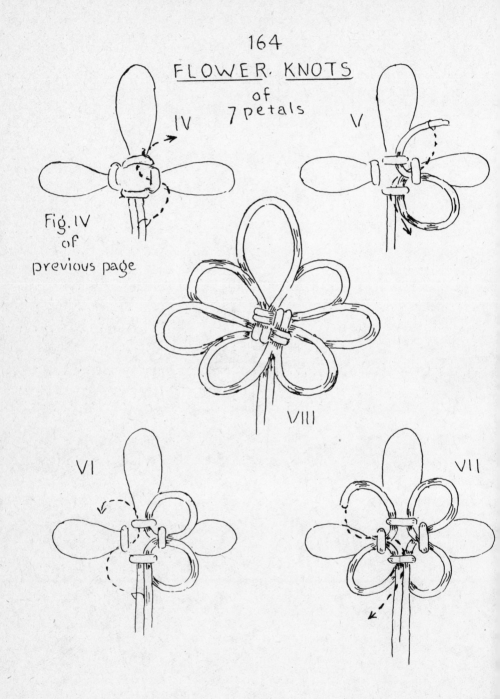

FLOWER. KNOTS
of
7 petals

IV

V

Fig. IV
of
previous page

VIII

VI

VII

CHRYSANTHEMUM

of
eleven petals

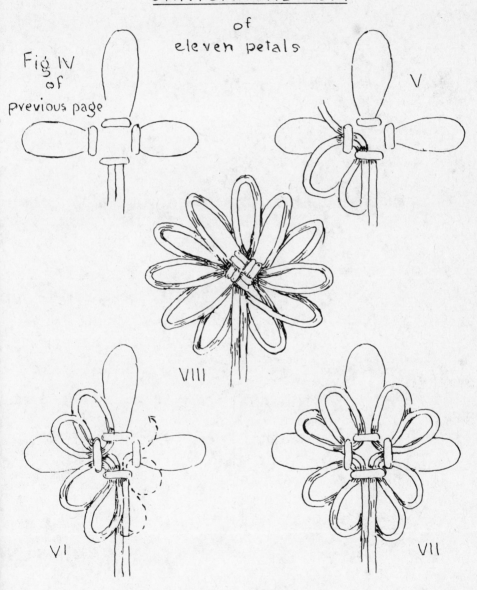

Fig IV
of
previous page

V

VIII

VI

VII

FLOWER <u>of</u> 3 Petals

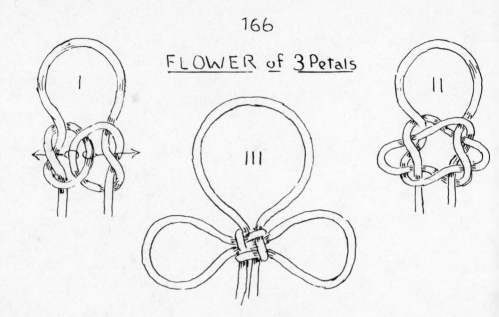

FLOWER of
5 Petals

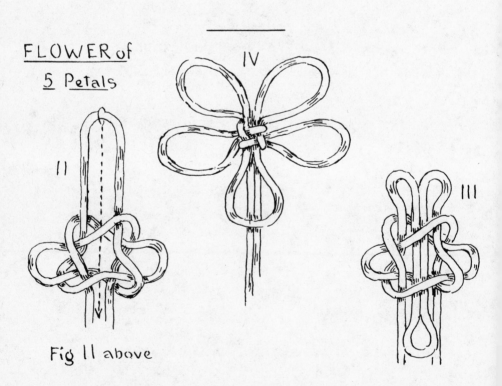

Fig II above

FLOWER
OF THE PLUM

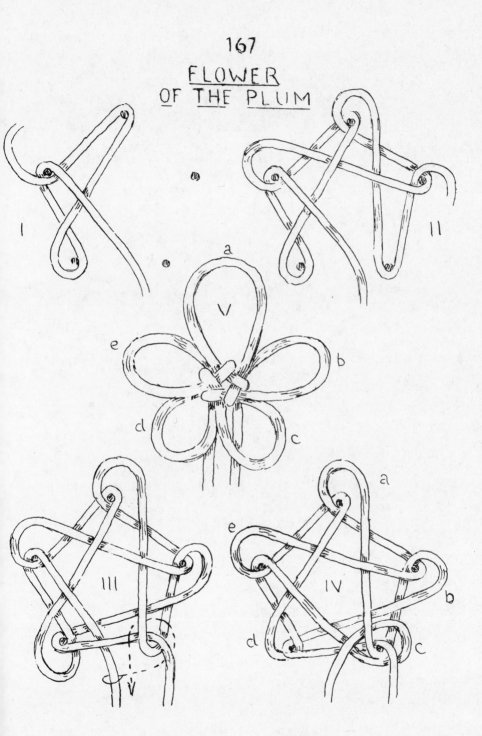

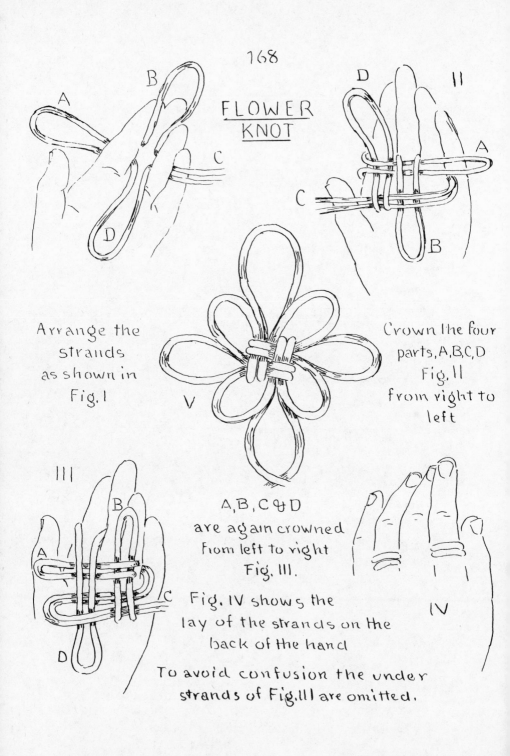

168

FLOWER KNOT

Arrange the strands as shown in Fig. I

Crown the four parts, A, B, C, D Fig. II from right to left

A, B, C & D are again crowned from left to right Fig. III.

Fig. IV shows the lay of the strands on the back of the hand

To avoid confusion the under strands of Fig. III are omitted.

POLYGONAL KNOTS

These Knots are
probably
of Chinese origin
They may be tied with the aid of
pins
placed at the angles
of
a triangle, square, pentagon
or other regular
polygon

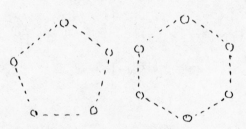

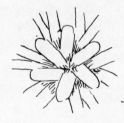

The radiating
strands
at the center of the knot
are double.
There is a top and bottom
layer
which are alike

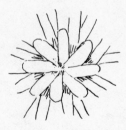

TRIANGULAR KNOT

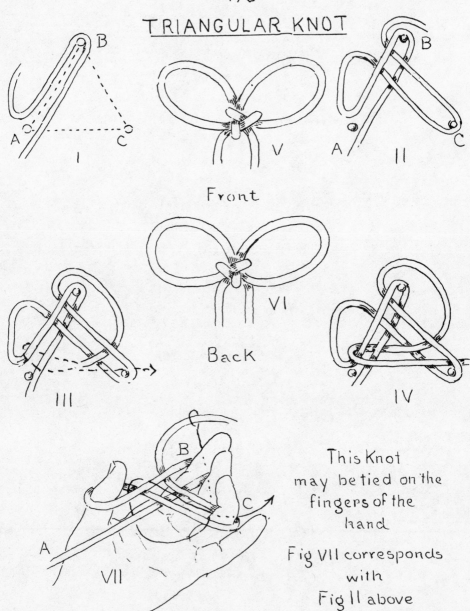

Front

Back

This Knot
may be tied on the
fingers of the
hand

Fig VII corresponds
with
Fig II above

171

DOUBLE
TRIANGULAR KNOT

Front

Back

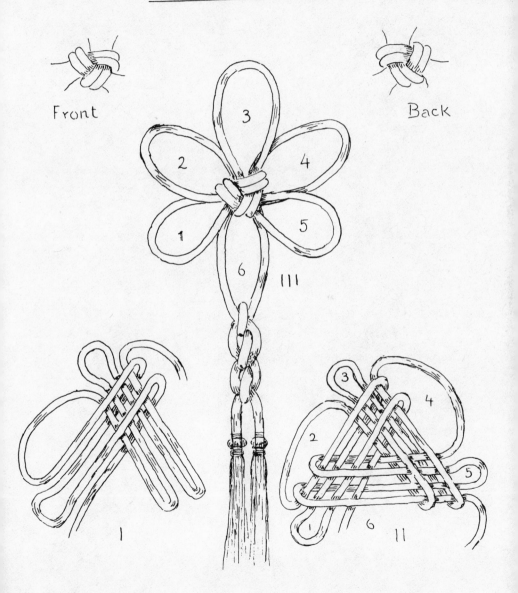

SINGLE
QUADRANGULAR - KNOT

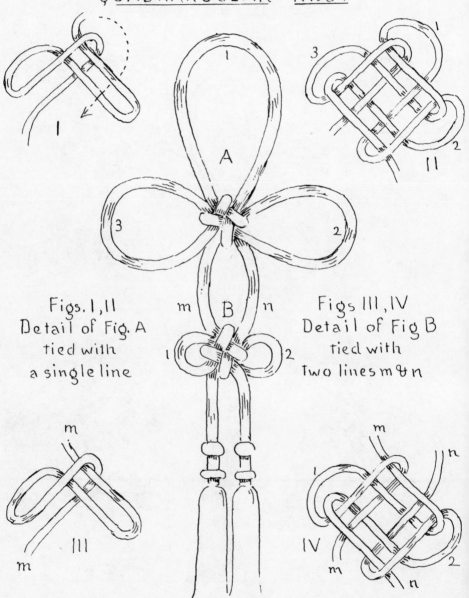

Figs. I, II
Detail of Fig. A
tied with
a single line

Figs III, IV
Detail of Fig B
tied with
Two lines m & n

173
DOUBLE
QUADRANGULAR-KNOT

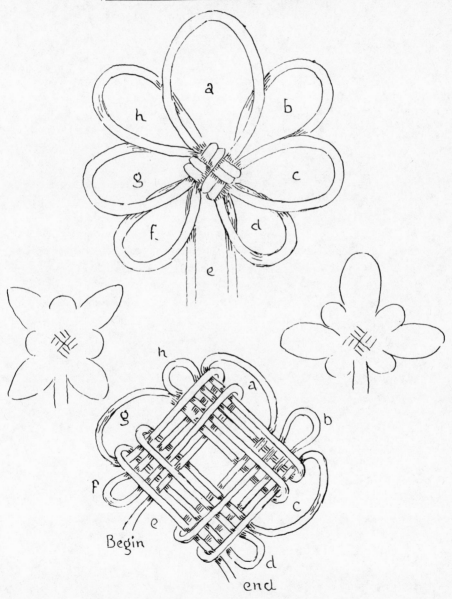

174
TRIPLE
QUADRANGULAR – KNOT

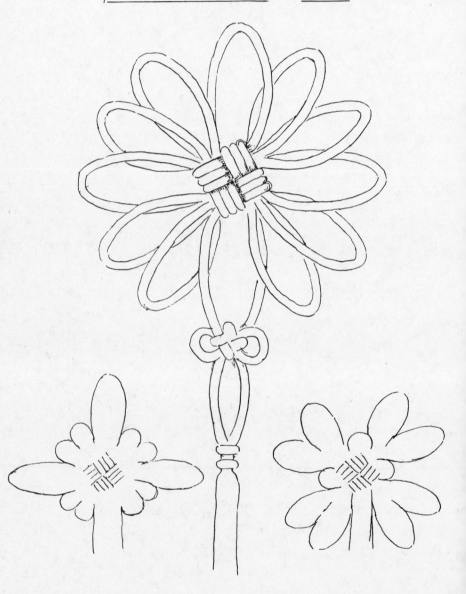

175

<u>DETAIL</u>

of the

Triple Quadrangular—Knot

The method is the same as that of the

single form

Figs. I, II, III and IV

<u>But</u> <u>with</u> <u>the</u> <u>loops</u> <u>in</u> <u>3's</u>

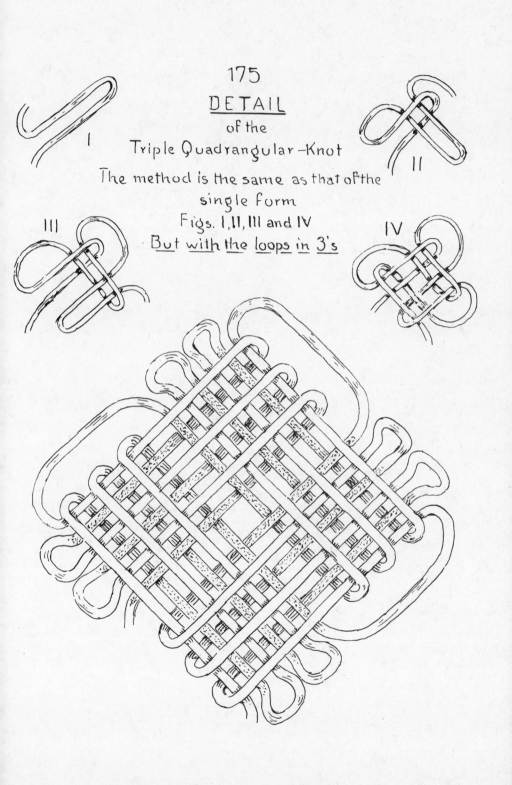

176

HEXAGONAL KNOT
Each Bight passes
through 2
Loops

177
OCTAGONAL KNOT
where
each Bight passes
through 2
Loops

DECAGONAL KNOT

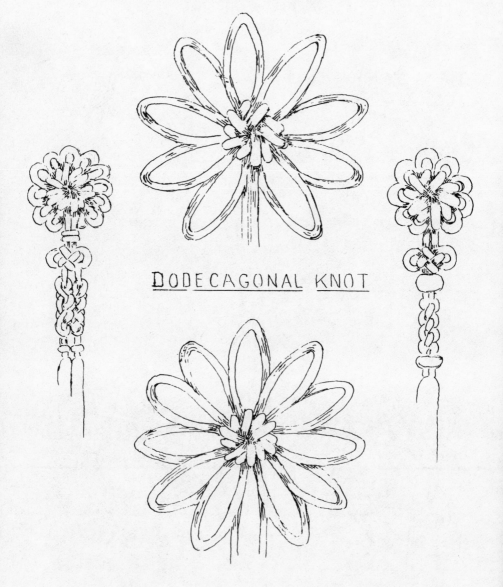

DODECAGONAL KNOT

DECAGONAL KNOT

Detail

Each Bight
passes
through 3 Loops

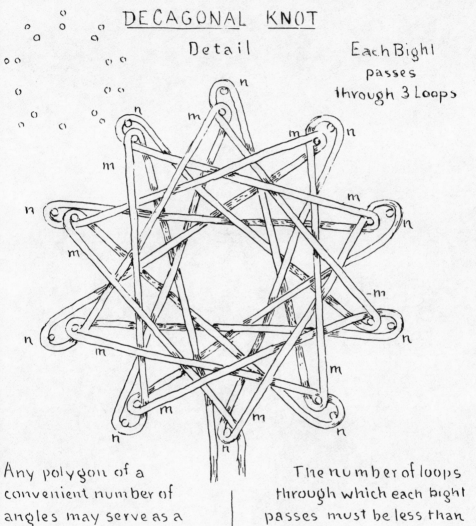

Any polygon of a
convenient number of
angles may serve as a
foundation for this Knot

The number of loops
through which each bight
passes must be less than
one half the number of angles

In adjusting the Knot
release all the bights m,m,m, ⊥ - -

pull gradually and equally all the bights n,n,n,---

180
CHINESE TASSEL

DOUBLE INTERLACING

These knots (probably Chinese)
are based on the
Quadrangular Knot
page 172

I

II

Fig. I shows
the upper and lower
strands,
the lower strands shaded

The number of strands in each layer may vary from
two to four, six or any convenient
<u>even</u> number

In the process of tying the knot, elaborations may
be introduced in which the Carrick Bend
appears, pages 185, 186, 188

A
diagram
with pins, that
correspond
with the number
of strands,
is necessary, also
pins to hold the strands
in place as the work progresses

A
cork board
6 or 8
inches square
is convenient for
this
and other intricate
Knots

182

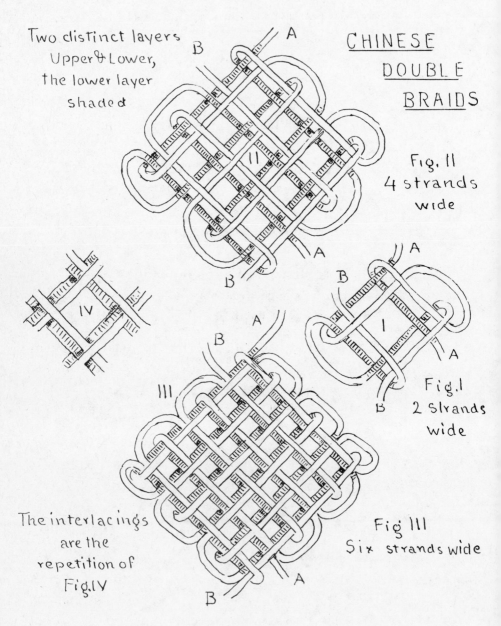

Two distinct layers
Upper & Lower,
the lower layer
shaded

CHINESE
DOUBLE
BRAIDS

Fig. II
4 strands
wide

Fig. I
2 strands
wide

The interlacings
are the
repetition of
Fig. IV

Fig III
Six strands wide

183

DETAIL

OF

Fig II on opposite page

A

I

A

A

II

A

B   A

V

B A

B   A

III

A

B   A

IV

B   A

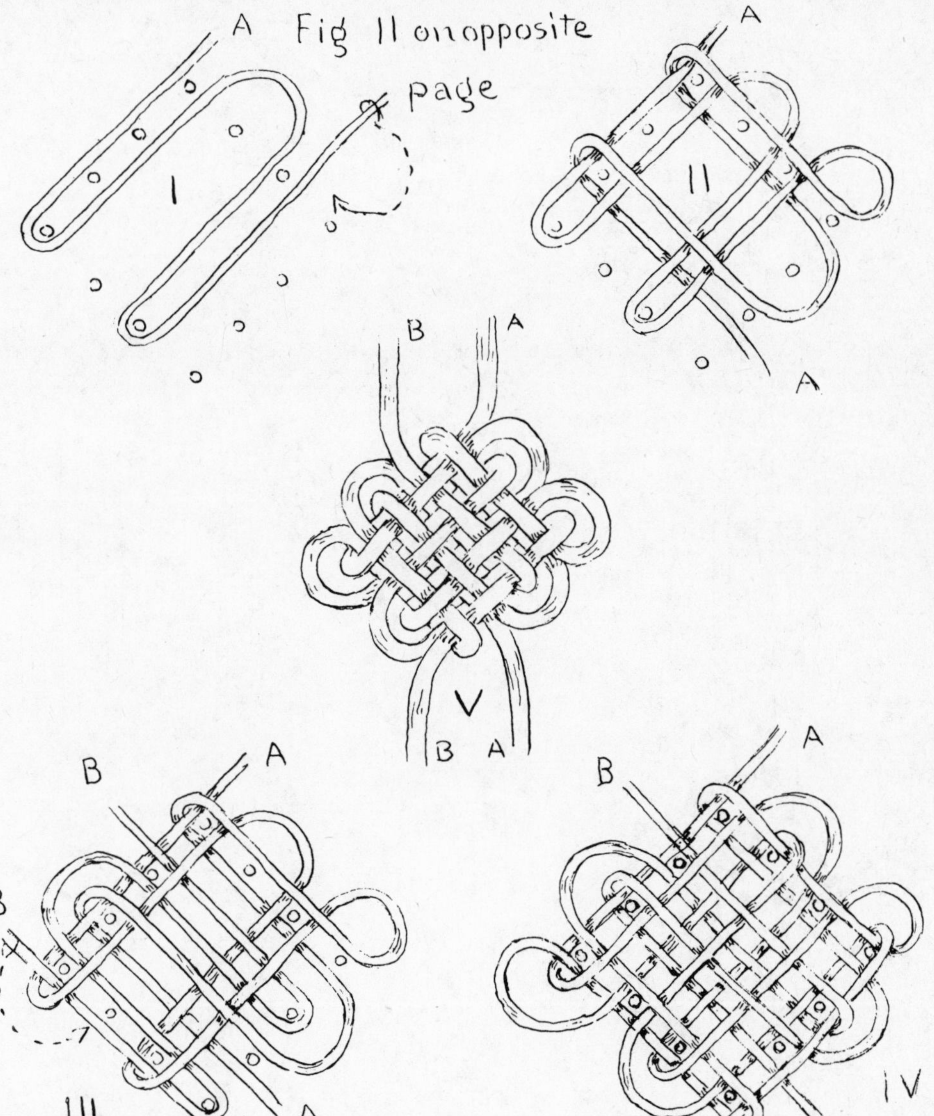

184

CHINESE
KNOTS

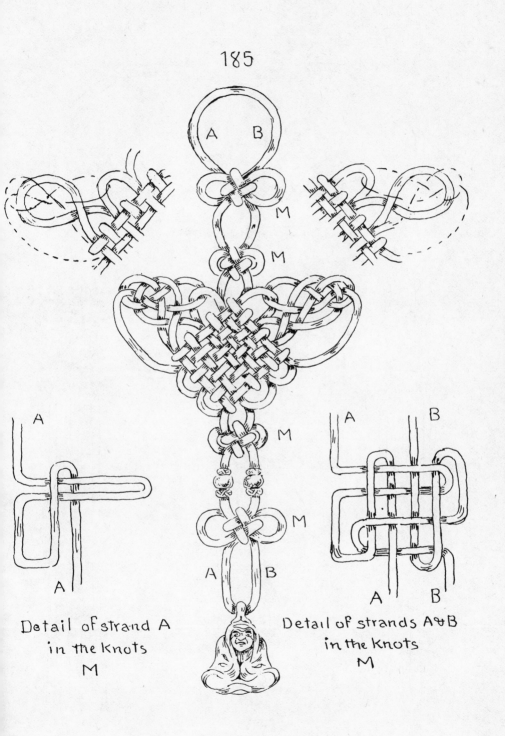

185

Detail of strand A
in the knots
M

Detail of strands A & B
in the knots
M

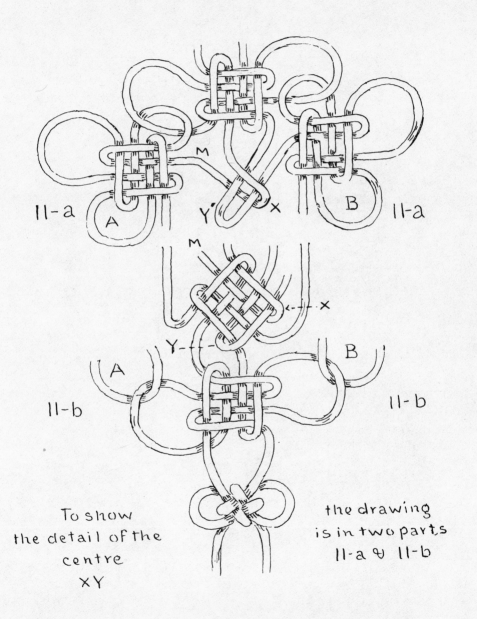

11-a

A

M

Y

X

B

11-a

11-b

M

A

Y - - - -

B

- - - - - X

11-b

To show
the detail of the
centre
XY

the drawing
is in two parts
11-a & 11-b

188
CARRICK BEND
and
CHINESE DOUBLE BRAID
in combination
Fig. I

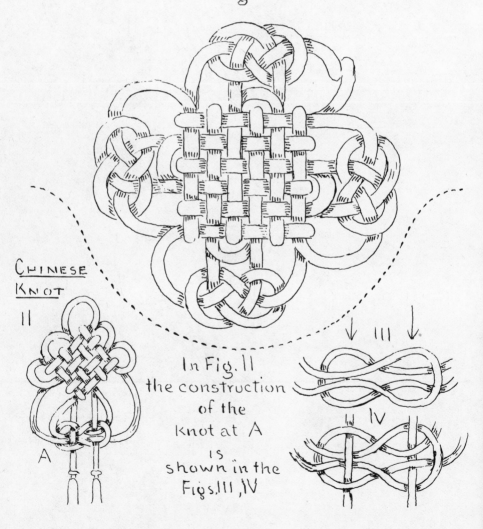

CHINESE
KNOT

II

A

In Fig. II
the construction
of the
knot at A
is
shown in the
Figs. III, IV

III

IV

TRICK KNOTS

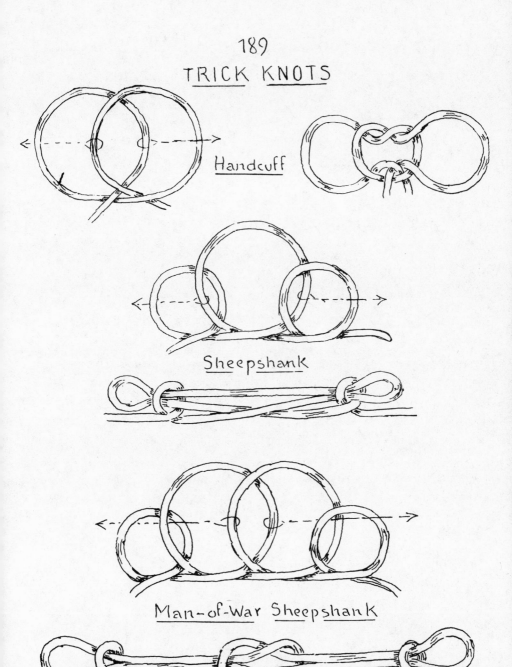

Handcuff

Sheepshank

Man-of-War Sheepshank

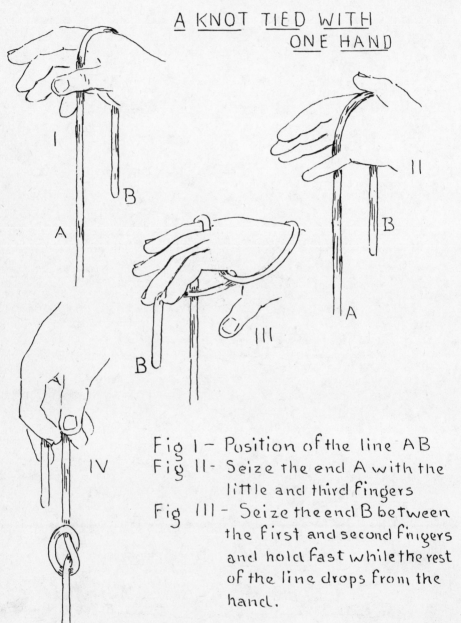

190

A KNOT TIED WITH ONE HAND

Fig I – Position of the line AB

Fig II – Seize the end A with the little and third fingers

Fig III – Seize the end B between the first and second fingers and hold fast while the rest of the line drops from the hand.

TRICK KNOTS

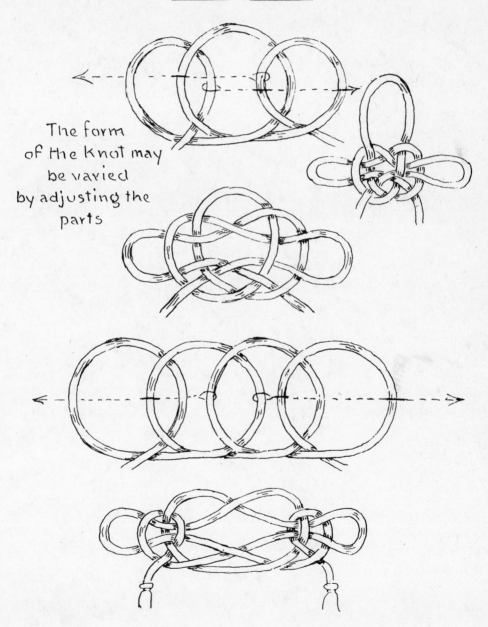

The form
of the knot may
be varied
by adjusting the
parts

192
JURY KNOT

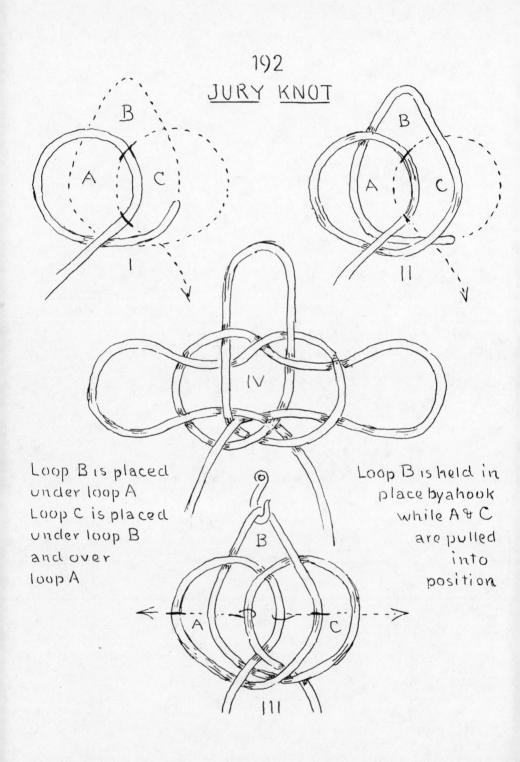

Loop B is placed
under loop A
Loop C is placed
under loop B
and over
loop A

Loop B is held in
place by a hook
while A & C
are pulled
into
position

TRICK KNOTS

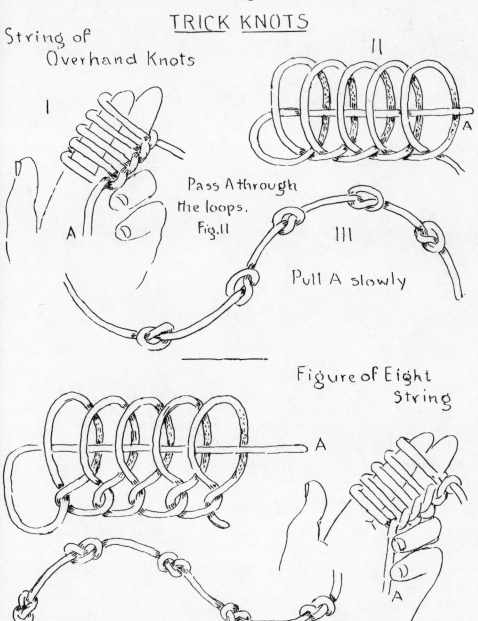

String of Overhand Knots

I

II

A

Pass A through the loops. Fig. II

III

Pull A slowly

Figure of Eight String

A

A

194

Adapted from the German